MW00932610

Therapist Practice
In a Box

SHERALYN L. SHOCKEY-POPE, LMFT

Text Copyright © 2017 Sheralyn L. Shockey-Pope, LMFT

All Rights Reserved

No reproduction of any portion of this publication or materials supplemental with this book is permitted without the permission of the author.

ISBN: 1548564338

ISBN-13: 9781548564339

Dedication

This book project is a labor of love and commitment to making the world a better place one therapist at a time. There were many hands and hearts that helped me with this project to make my dream a reality. However, before I ever wrote my first page, I had the unconditional love, support, and encouragement from the best person I know and love, Tracy Shockey-Pope, LCSW. Thank you for walking beside me through life and all the projects we have undertaken in our lives.

And to Kelsey and Trevor Pope, my adult children who provided me with laughter, suggestions, office work, ideas, and much love and support during this undertaking. You two enrich my life beyond belief.

I also want to acknowledge my parents, Felice C. Pope and the late Robert L. Pope, without whose bit of pushing when I was a teen, I would never have gone into counseling.

Thank you for all your support over the years. I love you all.

Disclaimer: Please note that this book and its contents should not be considered legal or tax advice. The information contained in this book and all Therapist Practice in A Box material is for educational purposes only. You should consult with an attorney, a CPA, or other professional to obtain legal or financial advice that will best meet your personal and business needs.

No reproduction of any portion of this publication or materials supplemental with this book is permitted without the permission of the author.

Acknowledgements

This book would have never gotten off the ground had it not been for my tribe of great therapists, friends, and co-workers. My first and foremost thank you must go to my wonderful, smart business partner, Jill Johnson-Young, LCSW, who helped me immeasurably by encouraging and courageously dreaming the dream of creating Central Counseling Services, Inc. with me because we wanted to help families with their problems and provide great value to our community. Our vision was and continues to be 1) To create a safe and nurturing environment for our clients and staff to thrive and grow and to be relieved of pain and suffering. 2) To reach back and teach and supervise interns who, in turn, will grow, learn, and share their awesome gifts with the world. 3) To welcome licensed staff with differing specialties to ensure we develop into a well-respected, diverse, and successful group practice for the good of our community. Thank you for taking that ride with me and sharing a passion for helping others. Also, thank you most of all, Jill Jonson-Young, for being my friend.

Table of Contents

Table of contents

Table of contents

"Having A Partner Definitely Allows You to Take More Risks."

Arianna Huffington, Co-Founder, The Huffington Post

Introduction

My Story

In 2008, my friend and current business partner Jill Johnson-Young, LCSW, and I were working for a local Child Protective Services agency. We both had been working there for many years, and our current assignment was in the adoption division. A large part of our job was developing and training foster parents, adoptive parents and "relative kin" families to be prepared to take the placement of children who had been removed from their parents and placed in foster care. As you can imagine, taking children away from their parents is never easy, and there must always be a serious and credible concern for the safety of the children before removal from their parents' care. Additionally, the act of removal can exacerbate the emotional damage done by the parents. The children who were referred to adoption program could not be returned to their parents for various reasons. During our employment, Jill and I kept hearing that these children were considered "RAD"— children who were diagnosed with Reactive Attachment Disorder. This particular diagnosis is very serious, and we felt that if any of "our children" were being diagnosed and labeled as RAD, it must be a mistake. Because, according to the Diagnostic and Statistical Manual of Mental Disorders (DSM) IV-TR, RAD is rare in the general population. Although there is a higher occurrence in the foster care population, the DSM and Mayo Clinic classify this as "seldom." Thus, we just didn't believe that our county could have a higher occurrence of RAD cases than the rest of the nation. There were just too many children in our county being given this diagnosis. In our work as county social workers, we received many phone calls from foster and adoptive parents asking for recommendations for "good therapists." The schedules of the "good therapists'" filled up quickly and it was not uncommon to hear that our clients had been "waitlisted." Frequently many parents we had worked with through foster care system asked, "Why don't you two open up a practice?" They wanted to refer their friends and family to someone that they knew, liked and trusted, namely, us. The concept of "know, like and trust" is the backbone of a good business.

Ethically, we knew that we could not provide therapy to these people while we were employed by the county. But their encouragement was a small spark. That spark grew. Then the fire was lit.

In 2009, out of frustration, but with a deep conviction to help others, we decided we should open a practice to see a few clients in the evenings and on weekends. When we decided to open the practice, the country was in an economic recession, but we reasoned, "Why not? People are always going to need help." Failure never occurred to us. After all, we knew we were competent, and we wanted to help others. While we had no real business knowledge, we knew how to respect people and how to conduct therapy. We had a passion for providing mental health services. We did not know exactly how to run a private practice. We just knew we were going to do it. As we talked more about starting this business, it became apparent that our graduate schools had not prepared us to run a small business. After about six months of research, we pooled together $10,000, rented an office, ordered business cards, threw up a website and scheduled our first clients. Our new clients saw our website or recognized our names and called us for appointments. We were officially in business by November of 2009.

Today, our company employs 13 to 15 clinical staff with various licenses and 3 nonclinical staff who run the office and complete special projects. Jill and I have been working full time since 2013 at our private practice, Central Counseling Services. I am happy to say we have made more money each year over the previous year, and every year since 2011 we have turned a profit and grown our bottom line. We are still looking for growth opportunities, and we may very well open a second location in the future.

Now, let's focus on helping you launch the practice of your dreams. The purpose of this program is to help you develop a plan to create your own successful private practice by clarifying and aligning your personal values with your business values in order to develop a niche early on. To that end, I have provided templates and checklists with action steps to help you get started. Are you ready to have some fun? Let's start building your private practice today!

Let's Start with Some Motivation

I always like to have a kick-off theme song for any project that I start. Often my motivation waxes and wanes and a "fight song" helps push me. I need a song that will motivate me when I am stuck and energize me when I start to slow down or burn out. This song must have a good beat, a positive message and be one with which I can sing loudly. Music for me is the pulse of life.

Introduction

Below are a few of my favorites. Look for songs that speak to you and adopt them. Sing loud and strong. Let me hear you. I know of no scientific evidence for this, but I think music helps us to work a little harder, pushes us a little longer and makes our journey a little easier. So, before you start your extraordinary project of practice building, go find your "fight song!"

20 Motivational Songs to Keep You Going

1. Don't Stop Believin'- Journey

2. Not Afraid- Eminem

3. Eye of the Tiger- Survivor

4. Rock You Like a Hurricane- Scorpion

5. Firework- Katy Perry

6. Let's Go- Calvin Harris & Ne-Yoh

7. Don't Stop Me Now- Queen

8. We are the Champions- Queen

9. Brave- Sara Bareilles

10. You Gotten Want It-Roberta Gold

11. You Get What You Give- New Radicals

12. Fighter- Christina Aguilera

13. Live Like We're Dying- Kris Allen

14. I Want to Be Rich- Calloway

15. How Do You Like Me Now? -Toby Keith

16. Stand Outside the Fire- Garth Brooks

17. Start Me Up- Rolling Stone

18. Stronger- Kelly Clarkson

19. It's MY Life- Bon Jovi

20. Tubthumping- Chumbawamba.

Bonus Tracks

21. Work Bitch- Britney Spears

22. Just Fine- Mary J. Blige

23. Survivor- Destiny's Child.

24. Shake It Off- Taylor Swift

25. Fight Song- Rachel Platten

Now add you own

26. _____

27. _____

28. _____

You probably want to know why I ask you to do something so silly. Well, it is so that you too can become extraordinary and do what you love. We all have a playful side. Let's use it. Having fun helps with being creative, so crank up that tune, do a little dance, and let the **Private Practice building begin!**

"And suddenly you know: It's time to start something new and to trust in the magic of beginnings."

—Meister Eckhart

Chapter 1: Let's Do This

Step 1: Creating the Right Mindset

So, you think you want to start a private practice, but don't know where to begin? Then this is the right book for you. In 2009, I had the same dilemma. I knew I wanted a group private practice; I just didn't know what it would look like or who I would be serving and helping. In the beginning, my business partner, Jill Johnson- Young, and I were somewhat fearful as to when to pull the trigger to start our business. Ultimately, we learned that once the basic structure was in place, it didn't really matter where we started, we just had to start somewhere.

Jill and I looked for an office, reviewed forms, and did marketing, one step at a time. My suggestion to you is to pick a starting point and put energy into it. Pick a starting date. How about today? You picked up this book, right? Well, that is a good start. Today is a good day for us to begin, even if it's only one baby step. Yup, today is a glorious day to start. Are you ready? Get set, here we go...! You are on your way to creating the successful private practice of your dreams.

Remember, no two practices will be the same. You are only in competition with yourself, despite the number of therapists in your particular market. You are unique and, a sad reality is there are plenty of people hurting in our communities who need our help. So, today is a grand day to start chasing your dream!

Step 2: Are You an Entrepreneur?

I hope you are already an entrepreneur. However, if you are like I was, with little to no experience, or idea of where to start, don't fret, you can learn these skills. Let's start with the basics: What exactly is an entrepreneur? The Miriam Webster dictionary defines an entrepreneur as "one who organizes, manages and assumes the risks of a business enterprise." So, if you are some type of healer, counselor, therapist, mental health practitioner or a student of such disciplines, and you have decided that you want a private business where you will practice your skills and talents, then you are, or will be, an entrepreneur. That is wonderful! I am so excited for you. I bet you are great at what you do.

How are your business skills? It becomes important to begin thinking like a business person. You must learn to market, network, and develop a business plan. If you are saying, "Yikes! Wait! No! I really just want to do therapy," then sadly, private practice is probably not for you. Look for a position at a community clinic, a hospital, a school, or other agency where you can go to work in the morning, see five to six clients a day, do great therapy, chart, and then go home at night. You can create a good life for you and your family by doing so. I did just that for many years. There is no shame in wanting to work in a stable financial environment or have an agency job. There are many advantages to this type of employment: steady paycheck, defined sick leave, vacation benefits, and many agencies have matching 401K retirement accounts. They also assign your caseload, do marketing, buy furniture, clean the office. In other words, the overhead is provided for, but if that is too comfortable for you and want or need a change, or you have decided you want a bit more, you can venture into the world of private practice. You need to look at your personality and be OK with working out of your comfort zone. When starting my practice, I had the passion for creating a business. My background was in Child Protective Services, a large government agency. This job provided the steady paycheck, steady clients, and a retirement account, but the work there became stagnant and stale. I was ready for and needed a change. At the County, I had limited input as to which clients I saw, the hours I kept, or projects I worked on. I got in trouble more than once for speaking up and not holding to the "party line." I wanted to have a say in decision making. I wanted to create my own hours and show up when I chose to. I wanted to take a risk and be the boss of me. My agency job had become too easy, too mundane. It was no longer satisfying. I wanted to push forward. I had a vision: I wanted to help people in a different capacity. For me, the agency work was no longer the positive challenge it had once been.

I'd been thinking about leaving the agency for over a year, and knew I needed a transition plan to make the private practice work and not lose money; after all, I had a family to help support. It took me almost two years to build up my private practice before I could leave the County, but I was determined. I started my practice part-time, working every evening and many Saturdays. Week by week my client caseload increased. I started adding vacation days from my agency job, used many holidays, as I worked towards going full time. During that transitional period, I read, asked questions, did research, explored options, and took on as many clients as I could. The word fail never entered my mind. My business partner and I never entertained failure as an option not once! We believed we would be successful no matter what, and we have been.

That is not to say we haven't made mistakes nor needed to learn new skills, and to gain knowledge to run a successful business. What I am saying is, for us, failing permanently and closing our doors was not an option. Period. We knew we would have ups and downs, but never would we shut down because we failed. We had worked for the government, and over the years we had developed resiliency, a tough work ethic, and tenacity, and those traits have served us well. We knew how to cope with lean years; we had already done that many times. *You* must start developing that mindset now. There will be rough times, but in the deepest part of your being, you must believe you will make it. You just must.

Traits of an Entrepreneur

The traits that I feel every entrepreneur should have or work on developing include: resiliency, focus, tenacity, hard work, vision, goals, ability to sell and persuade, and a burning desire to be successful. We all have some of these characteristics, and we can work on developing the ones that we lack. Remember, in the midst of it all this practice building, practice good self-care and self-compassion. So, do you want to be an entrepreneur? Does working hard and making your own schedule appeal to you? Do you want to work late nights and early mornings and still be able to see your child in the school play? Does working a nine to five job, Monday through Friday sound like torture? Would you be happier with a variable schedule of evenings and days? It will depend on how you schedule your time and how well you can get yourself organized as you develop your skills to become a great entrepreneur. Oh, and by the way, sometimes you will not be able to pay yourself on time, at least in the beginning. For me personally, being the boss of me works, but it does not work for everyone. You must think of <u>yourself</u> as the **Chief Executive Officer**. This means you will be in charge finding office space, getting the computers set up, ordering, fixing broken chairs, buying and using cleaning supplies, decorating and maintaining your office. In short,

<u>Everything is your job.</u>

Of course, you can hire help, but when we first started, we couldn't afford it. We painted the office ourselves in order to keep rent lower. When someone spilled coffee in the office, it was our job to clean it up. We no longer had the janitorial staff that came at night to clean the carpet, dust and wipes down everything. It was all on us—or my teenagers if they needed extra spending money. (Sometimes I would bribe them to come in for a day to help.) My business partner and I have wonderful extended families and friends who are handy with tools, tasks and are always willing to help.

Think about this type of a team. Who do you have that can help you? Find that team. It will make setting up a practice so much easier! Your practice is a business, and you must treat it accordingly. That means you will sometimes be uncomfortable. There are many decisions to be made, and sometimes you are just not sure what to do. Look to your team for help. I would often talk to my friends or family, not for them to decide for me, but to hear my own ideas out loud. Sometimes the ideas just couldn't be implemented, so, back to brainstorming.

Chapter 1: Let's do this

There are many skills you have, and there are those you lack If you do not have business skills, start developing them. They are skills, like everything else you have ever learned, nothing more, you can do this! Find your passion for creating your business.

A necessary skill is marketing. If you do not learn this, your ability to succeed will be diminished. When you work for someone else, you can show up, do your job, and go home. Essentially, you are working for someone else's dream. When you own your business, you are working on your dream and as such you must sell a product and/or service. You must learn how to persuade others to purchase your goods and services. You must become comfortable selling yourself and your practice. Practice getting out of your comfort zone. Take a few risks. You will be doing that a great deal in private practice. I do have good news: Everything I am telling you, can be done and be done well. I shall show you how to start, and after you practice it awhile, it will become easier. If all of this sounds exciting, then let's put on your new entrepreneur's hat and begin. Ready.... Set.... GO!

Step 3: What Type of Business Structure Do You Want?

Sole Proprietor

Do you want to be a sole practitioner? In this type of practice, you are the only clinician in the office, or you may work in the same office with other clinicians, but you are financially independent of each other. This is the simplest way to start a business. You own and manage the business 100%. You are responsible for all profits, debts, and liabilities. You make your own decisions, you choose the location, create business cards, logos, advertising, order office supplies, and you, *only* you, are the boss. As a sole proprietor, you own the business and can sell it at any time. You are also able to pass the business to your heir, providing they are a licensed professional or will hire licensed professionals to provide the services. The biggest downfall of this business structure is that you and your business are the same things: all financial risks are shared both professionally and personally. Yes, that does include your home, car, and first-born child. (Okay, I was kidding about the child part.) These assets can be sought after in a lawsuit or other legal procedure. The business entity you set up with the IRS may be your name, ex: Mary Smith, LMFT, or you can list yourself as an entity name, such as Sunset Counseling. (I will explain how to create a business without using your name later in the book.)

Group Practice or General Partners

Do you want a group practice like mine? Our practice, Central Counseling Services (CCS), began as a simple partnership. Later, we incorporated for tax and legal reasons. If you create a partnership, it is imperative to develop a partnership agreement. Talk to your potential partners about each other's strengthens and weakness and who is going to take responsibility for what tasks?

Who is going to complete the financials? Yes, this must be done. I know - you are a counselor, therapist, social worker, etc. I often hear "I don't do math." "That is why I became a _____, (fill in your career choice.)" You may hate math, but I bet you want to get paid. Someone in your partnership must do this task; figure out who and find a great bookkeeper or CPA to help with planning. In a group practice, you own a percentage of the company. The two or more partners

Chapter 1: Let's do this

together decide who to hire, where the office should be, how the paperwork will get done, etc. Are you going to hire more therapists or interns? Will they be a 1099 contractor or an employee? (I will talk more about this later in this book). In this type of practice, the skills you must have include being great at compromise and communication. Do you and the partners have the same vision? If not, how will you handle this? Please spell it out from the very beginning. There are risks with every structure, and for a group practice with general partners, the risks are like that of sole proprietorships. The income passes through to your personal taxes, but it's less costly and easy to set up (advantages). However, if you are sued and lose, your personal assets are on the line too. There are some operational and tax advantages, such as the ability to create a limited liability company (LLC), unless you are in California, then, you can't create an LLC for a professional business like ours. For more information on that, you can look up Moscone-Knox Professional Corporation Act. Also, in the next section, I shall describe different types of corporations.

This is how my partner and I started out, with a group practice. We wrote a contract making all things equal. We had the advantage of being long-time friends and knew already that we work well together. I never worry that my partner will do anything to put our company or ourselves at risk ethically, legally, or financially. A side note: Jill and I have a third partner who provided startup money and sometimes provides input to the practice, but she is not involved in the day-to-day operation nor does she draw a paycheck.

Are there other ways to form a company? I am so glad you asked, and the resounding answer is YES, my friend, there are.

Limited Liability (LLC)/Professional Limited Liability Company (PLLC)

This business entity is designed for licensed professionals, such as therapists, doctors, architects, accountants, chiropractors, and lawyers. The advantage of this type of business structure is that it is more flexible: It "limits" the liability and tax requirements, and there is a "pass-through" requirement, meaning each PLLC owner will carry the tax burden (profit or losses) onto their personal taxes. Additionally, owners can either be involved in the day-to-day management or can choose to hire managers to run the business. In many states, you are prohibited from owning an LLC, and instead, hold a PLLC to show the public you are a licensed professional. This is often called a hybrid, and it combines limited liability and has a better tax advantage.

PLEASE NOTE: If you are in California like I am, you cannot create your therapy practice as a PLLC or LLC. Enacted by the Moscone-Knox Professional Corporation Act, California Corporation Code Section 17375, 13401(a) and 13401.3, prohibits an LLC from rending professional services. California defines professional services as "any type of professional services that may be lawfully rendered only pursuant to a license, certification or registration authorized by the Business and Professions Code, the Chiropractic Act, the Osteopathic Act or the Yacht and Ship Brokers Act."

In the U.S., you can become a corporation. Each state has its own restrictions and guidelines. I have included a link to a great article by Nolo Press that details each state's requirements: *50-*

Chapter 1: Let's do this

State Guide to Forming a Professional LLC.
(http://www.nolo.com/legal-encyclopedia/forming-professional-llc/)

Corporations

Here again, we have choices. Remember, my private business started as a group practice with a simple contract. We later formed our corporation. We did this because corporations are regarded as their own entities, and the corporation pays its own taxes. The structure of a corporation is broken down into shareholders, directors, and officers.

Shareholders have certain liability protections and are not generally held responsible for business debts or other liabilities. Shareholders elect the Board of Directors, which may be your family or business partners. The Director and Board oversee the day-to-day business affairs. A corporation must file certain documents in its state and is governed by the state they are created in. A corporation can be either a C-Corp or an S-Corp (a tax determination). What determines which way to go depends on your business and taxes. An S-Corp is much like an LLC, which allows a pass-through of profit and losses to individual shareholders with certain restrictions. A C-Corp is often called "a double tax business," since it is taxed at the corporate level and the dividends are taxed at the personal level. C-Corps also allows for an unlimited number of shareholders, whereas S-Corps are limited to a maximum of 100 shareholders. Larger companies usually opt for forming as a C-Corp; small to medium-sized businesses often choose to incorporate as an S-Corp. Most therapy practices opt to be classified as an S-Corp, which is exactly what we did to reduce liability for each of us personally. When we changed our tax status from a general partnership to an S-Corp, it was based on taking on interns, how much money we made, and the advice of our tax professional.

Read through each type of business structure carefully and then select the one which makes the best sense for you. If you are asking my opinion, which you are if you are reading this book, please get the opinion of an attorney, CPA, or other professional, before you make the decision about your business structure.

When we first started our business, we couldn't afford the cost of creating an S- Corp. We were not making very much money, and to be honest, the whole idea of how to become a corporation, at that time, sounded just too daunting. We initially formed a group practice with three general partners for tax purposes. Bottom-line, pick one, solo, LLC/LLPC, or a group practice. Decide how much risk you are willing to take and still allow you sleep at night. Again, I would get the opinion of an attorney, CPA, or another legal professional before you choose your business structure.

BUSINESS STRUCTURES PROS AND CONS

SOLE PROPRIETOR
PROS

- Can make quick decisions.
- You are 100% in charge of all decisions.
- Simpler to set up.
- Less costly.
- Some creditors will extend credit due to unlimited liability.

- You and your business are one.
- Easy tax forms.

CONS

- All legal risks of the business are also yours personally.
- Can be lonely and you have less ability to consult.
- There is a great amount of work to be done and decisions to be made, and it's all on you.
- Subject to Self-Employment Estimated Taxes.
- Maybe hard to get a loan due to small size.
- High turnover rates of this type of business.
- File profits on personal taxes.

  TAX FORM: Schedule C 1040

PARTNERSHIPS GROUP PRACTICE

PROS

- Easy and inexpensive to form.
- Shared startup costs and financial commitment.
- Case consulting and collaboration.
- More specialists/niches
- Two or more people with skills and abilities.
- Can offer employment incentives to join the partnership.
- Practice with partners not as isolating.

CONS

- Busy practice and sometimes more noise and wear n' tear on furniture and office.

- Finding the right partners can be hard.

- Legal risk is yours and your partners.

- All are liable for one bad decision.

- You must trust your partners.

- Shared profits.

- Disagreements can occur.

- Differing work ethic and style.

TAX FORM: Schedule 1065

LIMITED LIABILITY COMPANY (LLC)

PROS

- The flexibility of being taxed as a sole proprietor, partnership, S-Corporation or C-Corporation.

- Protected from some or all personal liability if the company runs into legal issues or debts.

- LLC formed with one or many members.

- Simple flow-through taxation.

CONS

- Unable to use this structure if you live in California.
- LLC do not pay self-wages.
- More complicated to start and with higher fees.
- Multi members to run the business (can also be a pro).
- Harder to raise money.
- Less structure could lead to costly mistakes.
- Taxes passed onto owners.
- Self-Employment taxes.

TAX FORM: Schedule C 1040, like a sole proprietor.

CORPORATION

PROS

- Protects owners from liability.
- Formal business structure with duties.
- Ability to attract investors.
- Can continue if the Director or a shareholder dies.
- Independent legal entity.
- Can elect to become a C-Corp (IRS designation), eliminating double taxation.

Therapist practice in a box

CONS

- Costs more to start up.
- More time to set up.
- Must have a Board of Directors, articles of incorporation and annual meetings; more formal.
- Any shareholder that works for the company must pay themselves reasonable compensation.
- Stricter operational processes.
- More paperwork.
- Some double taxing.

TAX FORM: 2553 to elect "S" status 1120 or 1120-A

Resources

1. U.S. Small Business Administration

   https://www.sba.gov/business-guide/10-steps-start-your-business/

   The Small Business Association is a rich resource for information on how to set up a business. Their website has great articles on many business topics, and a newsletter you can subscribe to. Additionally, most of the information is free!

2. SCORE

    https://www.score.org/

    This non-profit organization of retired executives is the largest network of free business mentoring and services with great information.

3. The local Chamber of Commerce,other non-profit local business centers, and universities often are helpful resources.

4. Australian Government
    https://www.business.gov.au/info/plan-and-start If you live Down Under, the Australian government provides online guidelines on starting a business.

5. Legalzoom®

    https://www.legalzoom.com/

    A great place to help with business structure.

Check List of To Do Items

☐ *Start developing an entrepreneur mindset. Read a few business and marketing books and/or listen to podcasts.*

☐ *Pick your FIGHT Song.*

☐ *Start marketing! Tell everyone you know you are starting a business.*

☐ *I have the following qualities and skills, or I am willing to develop them:* ☐ *Ability to take risks* ☐ *Independence: the ability to trust my instincts* ☐ *Ability to negotiate* ☐ *I am persuasive* ☐ *A Visionary* ☐ *I can create a great support team.*

☐ *(if you do not have the above skills, start developing them now. These skills are like everything else you have ever learned nothing more.)*

☐ *Pick a business structure.*

☐ *Take a look at the Small Business Administration website, lots of valuable information.*

☐ *Pace yourself and practice good self-care. This process can take about a year.*

"There is only one way to learn. It's through action." — Paulo Coelho

Chapter 2: Nuts & Bolts

Step 1: Picking a Business Name

Now it's time to name your practice. This process can be stressful and time-consuming, yet exciting. Do you pick a name based on geographical located location: your city, a street name, or a name for the area of a larger city? Do you pick a name that makes you stand out, is bold, or trendy? I would suggest one that is easy to pronounce, spell and remember. I would also craft one that reflects your values and what you do as a clinician. First, sit down with a blank piece of paper (old school way) or a blank computer screen and list all the possible names for your business. Use it as a stream of consciousness exercise (the Freudian way). List all possible names from the most absurd, silly, from fun ones to conservative, serious ones. Look for a name that conjures up change, growth—one that defines your practice. Beware of double meanings or names that do not convey some sort of professionalism. I once had a friend name her therapy practice "Let's Talk." People were always surprised to find out she was actually a psychotherapist and not a speech therapist. She finally changed her business name when she got tired of explaining herself over and over again. Once you have a few names in mind, conduct a Google search to determine if anyone is using the same name. You do not want a name that someone else has used or is currently using. If that name is in use, cross it off the lists and move on. You don't want to have copyright or trademark infringement problems. That would be a huge time waster and could also be a costly problem. Lastly, do not make your name too long; you will be writing it often. Make this easier on yourself. You also can use your own name as your business name. Be sure to spell out your credentials and check your licensing regulation for your state.

In our practice we didn't want to use our last names because we felt, that sounded too much like a law firm, plus our names were just too long. We decided to take a vote. Each partner took a piece of paper and wrote down 10 names that yielded us 4 overlapping names. We mulled them over for a week, and thus, Central Counseling Services was born. I know what you are thinking, wow, you guys didn't stick to a short name. You are absolutely right; please learn from our mistake. We do use our abbreviation of CCS quite often.

Step 2: Domain Names

Once you have settled on a few original names, check to see if the domain name is taken. Go to a domain registrar, such as HostGator, and see if your business name can be purchased as a domain name. Try to find a business name and a domain that are similar or at the very least, can be branded together. Selecting your domain name is important, and it will take a lot of thought. Most short domain names have been already taken, so, you may have to get your creative brain working overtime. Domain names must be at least six letters long. If possible, try to get your domain name as a .com. as your ability to be found in a web search is greater if you have a .com name. A .net is a good second choice. If you are a sole proprietor in structure, the business name often includes your first and last names and getting a .com is easier. Remember: If you are using any name other than your legal name, you also must submit a Fictitious Name Filing, more about that later in this book.

In selecting our domain names (we have multiple websites) we try to stay as close to our name as possible. It makes it easier to remember.

A few more pointers

➢ Use your business name for your domain name or use your niche specialty or location, such as city name and "Counseling."

➢ Try to find your potential business name and a domain name with the ".com."

➢ If you use "Associates" in your business name, for example, "Smith Counseling and Associates," you may have to file a Fictitious Business Name with your county and/or state. This document must be filed if you are using any name other than your legal name.

➢ Look for domain names that are easy to spell; avoid the letters "Q," "X" and "Z." They get confused with other letters and are hard to pronounce. (There are plenty of exceptions to this rule, e.g., Quiznos, Sandwich Shoppe, Xerox, and my friends at Zynnyme.com, a great company that helps therapists build better practices (more about them later).)

> ➢ Don't use hyphens or numbers in your domain. Google and other search engines don't like them, and these affect your Search Engine Optimization (SEO) ranking. (The higher the SEO ranking, the more people will be able to find you.)

Step 3: Where to buy a domain name

There are plenty of domain name registers around, such as Namecheap, Bluehost, Hover, and Hostgator. I personally use Namecheap for domain names and Bluehost for my hosting service. They are easy to manage and maintain and are not very expensive. Regardless of which one you choose, be sure to purchase a domain name that represents you and your business.

TIP: When you start to register your practice and sign up for the directories and other websites, like White Pages, each will require you to have a username and password. Because there are many to remember, I recommend a "password manager," a program that stores all your passwords securely and safely. It also will generate secure passwords with special characters of various lengths to satisfy the pickiest of websites. The best part is you only have to remember one password, and it will remember all the rest. They have a free version I would try first. I started with the free version of LastPass and then upgraded when my needs have changed. However, I also use the paid version for my telephone it costs about a $1.00 per month.

Step 4: Let's Look at Funding

my business partner and I decided to open our therapy practice, we pooled $10,000 and hoped that it would be enough to create our business. We discussed our vision thoroughly and knew we eventually wanted to give back by having space in our office for a few interns and some licensed therapists. However, we had to start small. We created a budget and knew we had to stick to it.

What if you don't have that kind of personal money to invest? Here are some options:

➢ Bank funding. You may be able to take out a personal loan depending on your personal FICO score. Because your business doesn't have credit yet, the banks require you to guarantee the loan.

➢ Personal savings. This might be an option if you can save a certain amount each month from your day job.

➢ A "side hustle" job. A "side hustle" job. The Urban Dictionary describes a "side hustle" as a "sideline that brings in cash; something other than your main job, maybe playing weekend gigs or life coaching." This "side hustle" could also be a passion of your that you do. A friend of mine, an accountant, bakes gluten-free dog treats on the weekend. He takes them to local fairs and pet expos. He uses his extra money to invest in his business. For inspiration and ideas, check out *99 Side Hustle Business Ideas You Can Do Today* by Side Hustle Nation, http://www.sidehustlenation.com/ideas/.

➢ Defer money by not take a salary from your private practice for a few months. Use your day job to fund this new business. We did this on occasion when our cash flow was lean. I am happy to report that for many years we have paid ourselves a living wage. You will be able too as well, once you build up your clientele. But be prepared to dip into your personal funds or just not pay yourself for a little while.

➢ Look for "outside investors." Do you have a relative or good friend who might be willing to fund you for a while? I only "tongue-in-cheek" suggest Shark Tank since they probably wouldn't be interested in funding a psychotherapy practice nor would they be able to get their money back quickly. Mr. Wonderful would say he can't see how to scale up your business; a Shark Tank investment is not likely. It doesn't take too much money to get started. It's worth considering some outside source.

➢ List all your ideas on paper even the most far-fetched. You will never know if you just might find a funding source.

Step 5: Licenses and Permits

To run a business, you will also need to acquire the proper licenses and permits. The type you need will vary by state, city, and even by industry. However, most therapy practices will need at least a business license. In California, I must pay for a City Business License, then pay taxes to the county for my business equipment. They then provide me with a permit. Research your local area's requirements. Do not run your business without a license; the fines can be very steep.

I have a few therapist friends who run their practice out of their home. This is then considered a home-based business and sometimes will require a business license.

Step 6: Getting a Fictitious Business Name (FBN)

What is a Fictitious Business Name?

The Small Business Administration defines a Fictitious Business Name (FBN) as "Doing Business as Name (DBA)." "A fictitious name is an assumed name, a trade name or DBA name. This name is different from your personal name or the names of your partners. For example, when I started my business, Jill and I decided on "Central Counseling Services," an FBN as our DBA.

If you are an LLC or Corporation in business structure, this step is not necessary as it is done when you file; the legal paperwork needed to create such business entries and an FBN is automatically filed. Please note: Not all states require an FBN.

When you use your legal name as your business name, an FBN isn't an issue. If not, however, you must sign up for a Fictitious Business Name. For example, if Samantha R. Timpson uses "Samantha R. Timpson, LMFT" as her business name, she does not need to file for an FBN. However, if she uses "Sam's Counseling Company" or "ST Therapy Group," she will need to file for a fictitious name.

Pretty much anytime you're not using your legal name; you must have a fictitious name statement. As a general partnership doing business under "Central Counseling Services," I was required to file an FBN.

The Process

This step is fairly easy, low cost, and can often be completed at the local county's administration building or county services center. A few states may require you to file at the state level; you can call your local Chamber of Commerce if you are not sure. The process goes something like this. You do a county or State search at the for your business name to see if it is already in use. If there is nothing recorded in that name, you then fill out the forms required with your personal information and pay the filing fee. Next, publish your name in the business section of the local newspaper. Shop around; this can cost a lot in larger newspapers; smaller papers often offer the service for around $30.00. There should be a list of acceptable newspaper offered by your agency. This legal notice is published once a week for four weeks after you file the affidavit that is published along with a copy, stamped by the newspaper, and the state or county grants you a Fictitious Business Name Statement.

Step 7: Acquiring an IRS Tax Number: Employer Identification Number (EIN) in United States

All U.S. businesses should have a specific Tax ID Number or Employer Identification Number (EIN). This number is assigned to your business and will be different from your personal social security number. An EIN is given to every company that you do work for and pays money to you for your services, such as insurance companies and grant providers. Also, this number is used for consulting work, and will be required on clients' "superbills," a statement for them to submit to insurance. You want to protect your personal social security number and not provide it to any clients. The EIN is the number you can safely give them.

I would suggest even if your business structure is a sole proprietor business, please get an EIN and do not use your personal social security number. The good news is, it is easy to apply for this number online at the IRS website: http://1.usa.gov/1oGE5Ot. When you apply for a number, know the type of structure your business will use. You can use your home address or a post office box at first if you don't have physical-office address and change it as soon as you have a business location. You will receive a document called an SS-4 from the IRS. It proves that the IRS has granted you a number. Save that document in a safe place. You may need to prove your number to banks, payroll services, and insurance companies. If you change your business structure at any time, as we did from a general partnership to a corporation, you will need to go back and get a new EIN.

Other Countries If you are a business in the European Union, you may need to apply and use a Value Added Tax (VAT) number. To complete the compliance process, check out http://www.vatlive.com/country-guides/ and by registering with HM Revenue & Customs (HMRC) https://online.hmrc.gov.uk/registration.

If you are in Australia, go to its government website. Gather information on Australia Business Number (ABN) and Goods and Services Tax (GST) at https://www.business.gov.au/.

Chapter 2: Nuts & bolts

For Canadian friends, her is a great article on what you need to start a business. https://www.thebalance.com/canada-business-tax-id-number-2948590/

Pointers:

> ➤ The IRS (USA) will give you a form called an SS-4 that lists your EIN. This is the official document that the IRS provides to prove that an EIN is yours and what your official business name is. You may be required from time to time to prove that number is official, so keep that page handy.
> ➤ I keep all important paperwork such as my SS-4 in a notebook that I can easily find. You will need to use this document at the bank, for city permits, and with many insurance companies. I once had an insurance company that I was not "paneled with," ask for a copy of my SS-4 before they would pay its member the fee from the superbill.

Check List of To Do Items

☐ Choose a business name.

☐ Buy a domain name.

☐ Arrange for funding for your business: from where, how much will you need?

☐ Decide to work your full-time job only or also a "side hustle" job?

☐ Find an accountant or business attorney to provide guidance.

☐ Create a legal business structure.

☐ Find out what permits and licenses you will need.

☐ Set up a password manager. (There are too many passwords in the world to remember.)

☐ Register a fictitious business name, unless you are filing for a corporation, then this will be part of the process.

☐ Get an EIN.

☐ Look for classes, workshops, resources, and information in your area such as a local Chamber of Commerce, Small Business Association, a women's business center, and a SCORE group.

Chapter 2: Nuts & bolts

☐ *Go to networking and business networking groups get to know at least three people from each event.*

☐ *Self-care, this is a must. Please always plan it into your daily schedule.*

☐ *Talk to your friends about your new business.*

To the world, you may be just one person, but to one person you may be the world. —*Brandi Snyder*

Chapter 3: The Plans

Step 1: What is Your Niche?

Now that you have the legal ability to start a business, you need to focus on developing your niche or specialty. When I ask my interns what they might want as a niche, they frequently stare blankly at me and say, "I don't know." They further say they have no idea how to develop one. Now, that may also be true for you. So, I ask you, what kind of clients do you want to treat?

What Type of Clients Do You Want?

Think about this for a moment. What clients do you feel you have a great understanding of? What clients get you energized to see and work with? Do you have clients that you look forward to seeing; those you feel a real connection with?

Let's do an exercise right now, yes, now. Take a moment. Close your eyes and think about all the clients you have seen. Pick the top three or four clients you most enjoyed working with. What do they have in common? Which ones did you feel you understood the best?

Those types of clients are the ones for whom you should start developing a niche. Think about your "why" for becoming a counselor. Does that impact who you like to work with? Did

Chapter 3: The plan

you become a therapist because your best friend in high school had anxiety?

Questions to Ask Yourself

Once you have honed in on the clients you like to work with, write down everything you can about those clients. If you are just starting, or don't currently have a strong preference, you can always zero in on your clients as you work with them over the next few months. Start thinking about it *now* and ask yourself these questions:

1. What clients do I totally understand?

2. What type of client leaves me exhausted after a session?

3. What type of client leaves me full of energy?

4. What type of client when I look at my schedule I look forward to seeing?

5. Is working with children using play therapy or sand tray a fun way to spend time with a client?

6. Do I fully understand teens? (*does anybody?*)

7. What about couples? Is that what you enjoy working with? Can you hardly wait to take on a fighting couple?

8. Does the depressed mommy-crowd get me going?

Frequently Asked Questions (FAQs) by Clients

Once you have narrowed down your specialties, think about what questions are most frequently asked by those particular clients. What theme come up during the sessions? What are the common words that clients use to describe their problems? What are the concerns that your clients bring about their problems? Start thinking about the symptoms the client is concerned about. For example, if clients come to you for anxiety, some questions that the clients may ask about anxiety are:

1. Are panic attacks normal?

2. Do you think I am having a heart attack or is it just panic?
3. Is it normal to have these thoughts going around and around in my head?

If your specialty is parenting, your list might look like this:

1. Will I always feel overwhelmed by my children?
2. What if I don't like my children?
3. Am I a bad mother?
4. Why does my child lie?

Develop a handout of 10 Frequently Asked Questions (FAQs) about your niche. Post this on your website. Blog about each one on the list and post, then put the blog on your website. You might even develop another handout that you can give to your clients on the techniques they can use. These top ten questions come from your clients. These are the questions they are asking you during sessions. All you need to do is pay attention to what

Chapter 3: The plans

they are asking. There will be themes and certain questions that you are often answering for them. Write them down.   Creating this list can help you address their pain.

Once you have this information, you begin to write your website copy, addressing the symptoms and provide how you can help your client. Also, you can become more detailed in blogs you write about their problems. Use their words, show them that understand them. Also, use your social-media posting to link back to these blogs and your website.

This will help you keep marketing costs down. The more you use your client's language and demonstrate your knowledge of how you can help, your expertise in that area will grow. You will start being known for your specialty. Plus, if you are only marketing to a couple of niches, that marketing becomes more specific, and thereby, less expensive to acquire a new client. I hope you are seeing the trend of finding the right clients for yourself and its relationship with targeted marketing for your business.

Tip: Be sure to brand any handouts (or PDFs) you create with your name, phone number, and logo. Your clients may want to share it with family or friends, make it easy for them to contact you.

All therapists should have general knowledge and the ability to treat depression, anxiety, substance abuse, etc. Nevertheless, if the depressed mommies drag you down, then that is the client with whom you do not specialize nor to whom you market to.

To make it long-term in this field, you should see the clients that you fully understand. I know you are saying, "But I want to treat all clients and I don't want to limit my practice!" Really? Do you go to the general surgeon if you need orthotics for your shoes? Of course, not.

Be mindful and taking time with all potential clients to get a good understanding of what they want help with. I have offered referrals when clients are not a good fit for me. I will often refer out to a local therapist (Another good reason to network).

Sometimes clients are just not ready for therapy when they make that first call. I have had potential clients decline services for a variety of reasons, only to call me back a couple of months later and want to set up an appointment. They say they called me back because I was so helpful to them that first time we spoke, even though they didn't come in then.

Number of Clients: Your Caseload

The actual number of clients you need at any one time may surprise you. You only need about 30 to 40 clients seeing you within a month to make it financially. Your caseload will sometimes vary as clients will cancel when they are sick, go on vacation or are transitioning out. However, if you see on average 20 to 30 clients a week, you can make a decent living. Therefore, you don't need hundreds of clients all at once and knowing this should take some of the pressure off.

Become an Expert

You will attract more clients if you start to specialize and focus your energy and training. It will also save you money because your marketing will be focused. That being said, start becoming an expert in the areas where you want to specialize. Read as much as you can on the subject. If you are currently in graduate school, research areas of interest. It has been said that an expert is someone who has about 10,000 hours of research and experience with one particular topic. Start developing that now, no matter where you are in this process.

Create Your Avatar Client

Chapter 3: The plans

It's time to start to create your avatar. What the heck is an avatar? I first heard this term from John Lee Dumas of the wonderful podcast "EO Fire." Essentially, an avatar is a make-believe or invented person that embodies the culmination of your ideal client. The avatar is so descriptive that they seem real enough to have a conversation. This is the "person" you will be writing to when you are writing your emails, blogs, and sales letters. This is the person to whom your website or videos must speak. What problems of this "person" can you help him or her solve? What areas of concern or complaints does this person have that you can assist? You must know that person so well that you see them in your mind's eye. What goes into an avatar?

Below is a short list. Feel free to add more.

- ➢ Gender
- ➢ Age
- ➢ Occupation
- ➢ Life Circumstances
- ➢ Income
- ➢ Biggest frustrations
- ➢ History
- ➢ Aspiration
- ➢ TV shows
- ➢ Magazines
- ➢ Goals

Therapist practice in a box

- ➢ Interests

- ➢ Top 3 Fears

- ➢ 3 Values
- ➢ Married, with or without kids

The more detailed you can become the better you can target that person and help them. See why you can't have 13 niches, and you need to focus your energies? Try to aim for say 50 to 75 items about your ideal client. (Okay overachievers, write 100.) Focus on where they hang out and how to help eliminate their pain. What do they worry about? Think about what they like. Where do they go? What do they read? What do they do for fun? How do they describe their problem? What is their favorite music? The more you know what your ideal client, the easier it will be to connect with them in your writing for the blog and website. Take the time to write it out. Knowing your ideal client makes marketing to that client easier and less costly.

TIPS

- ➢ Attempt to be known as the go-to therapist for: couples, trauma, teens, children, or fill in the blank_____. That is the main goal.
- ➢ Think about with what type of clients you like to work and think about blog topics that will interest those clients.

- ➢ Remember what your clients ask when they come to see you? Write those 10 F&Qs down. You can start this even in your practicum training. Keep a running list of what clients ask you and what words they use.

➢ Develop no more than a couple of specialties. It will be easier to develop one at a time. But go ahead, overachiever, I know you are reading this and taking it as a challenge, and you will do 2.

Step 2: Write Blogs

I can hear you, "What? I don't even have a practice yet!" That is okay. You still have the knowledge, and you are developing skills that need to be shared with the world. You need to build up your credibility and having your name out there is helpful. You will share these blogs on your website, which will help with your SEO, which again stands for Search Engine Optimization. This is the big search engine that helps Google and Bing and others find your website. The higher you rank in the search results, the easier it will be for the right clients to find you. Another benefit to writing blogs is, with most skills, the more you write, the better you become. Start writing now. I will talk more about blogging later in the marketing section of this book, but it's a good idea to start developing your voice now, today. Start out slow, but every time you have even an extra hour, think about putting some content out there for your ideal client to get to know you.

Step 3: Business Plan

"What the heck," you say. "I don't even have a business yet. What is a business plan and why do I need one? No more work! I want the fun of designing business cards." Relax. We will get you cards, but first, you need at least an outline of what your business should look like, a vision of what you want to create. This does not have to be a gigantic work plan, but you should have an outline of your business. Please think of this as a living document, a blueprint or template to help you plan your business for this year, three years from now, and five years from now. This document will change and grow as you and your business change and grow.

I know it's not a lot of fun, but it's necessary to have the picture and plan. Dream in this step; dream big, play big, yes, big, big, BIG. This world needs you. Take the time to do this well, please. Note that you will change things. You will not hit every goal or target, and that is okay. You may redefine the goals more in detail later.

Sample Business Plan

Here is a **sample business plan**, with the items you will need to include in your document. Substitute You Got This Counseling Center (YGTCC) for your business name.

1. COMPANY SUMMARY

Think about your values and how you want the world to see you. The You Got This Counseling Center (YGTCC) is a mental and health counseling/education center focusing on foster care children, youth who have problems with their parents, and senior citizens with mental health issues, such as dementia and Alzheimer's. YGTCC is located at or will be in downtown Riverside, CA. The owner's investment is $6,000 (or whatever you are investing). We will set ourselves apart from the competition with our personal touches, like a calming and inviting office, clear and concise forms, snacks in the waiting room, an array of magazines, etc. *(Dream it, see it, write it down!)*

The keys to success for this business will include:

➢ Marketing

➢ Community reputation

Chapter 3: The plans

- ➢ Service excellence

- ➢ Growth potential (growth projections)

- ➢ Monthly positive cash flow

- ➢ Efficient office (electronic Medical records?)
- ➢ A safe, calm, professional counseling center

- ➢ A serious for-profit business

2. SERVICES:

YGTCC will provide the following services:

- ➢ Individual therapy

- ➢ Couples therapy

- ➢ Family therapy

- ➢ Group Therapy: We will have two groups a month

  1. Co-parenting Group

  2. Caregiver's Support Group

In Year 2

We plan to offer at a higher cost, in-home counseling services. It is our hope that we can provide 20 sessions a month, thereby generating higher revenue.

In Year 3

We expect to expand to ten clinicians and increase our groups to two teenage and two senior groups. We will become consultants and create products. *(Will you teach, lecture or create products? Vision it, build it, put it on paper and get it into the universe. What forms of income will this business have? It will happen.)*

3. **Ownership:**

You Got This Counseling Center will be a privately-owned corporation. (State your business structure. If you have a loan or have silent partners that invested money, list them here.)

4. **Business Operations:**

YGTCC will provide services from 9:30 AM to 8:00 PM, Monday through Friday, and 8:30 AM to 3:00 PM on Saturday.

➢ The staff of five therapists will divide the available hours.

➢ Insurance will be verified before the initial visit, and the co-pay will be collected.

➢ Treatment plans and case notes will be completed on the same day of service, or within the next business day, on rare occasion or circumstances.

➢ A billing sheet will be provided to the billing staff within 24 hours.

> ➤ If the client is paying by credit card, it will be processed the day of service.

> ➤ Cash payments will be deposited by the close of business.

Think about general policies for how you want to handle your business. Remember, these aren't set in stone and can change when you need them to. All you need right now is a starting point.

5. MARKET ANALYSIS SUMMARY:

Our company is located in Riverside, California with a population of 303,871. In California, the population is 38.6 million and is expected to grow approximately 50 million by the year 2020. The elderly, defined as 60 and older, is expected to grow at twice the rate of the total population. It is projected that in Riverside County the growth of the elderly population will increase by 200%. One of our target populations at YGTCC is senior citizens with Alzheimer's or

other dementias. We shall outreach to this population of 40,000 potential clients by speaking at local senior centers and health fairs. We also shall reach out to local senior housing programs and offer information, counseling services, and groups ~~we~~ that can be done in the community. We shall supplement the information through blogs on our website, guest blogs, and videos. Additionally, we shall network with primary care physicians (PCP) to increase resources for this population.

Therapist practice in a box

Our local competitors include: 16 therapists in the City of Riverside and 13 therapists within a 10-mile radius. Within this group, four of these therapists work for me, nine of them I know, and four work only part-time. This is not enough therapists for the 40,000 elders in this city. Our numbers are validated by the Institute of Medicine (IOM) and Substance Abuse and Mental Health Services Administration (SAMHSA) study. According to the IOM and SAMHSA report, there is an insufficient supply of trained professionals available to provide mental and behavioral health services to older adults. Additionally, according to the (APA) American Psychological Association data on the elderly as of 2015:

- ➤ An estimated 20.4% of adults age 65 and older met the criteria for mental disorders, including dementia, during the previous 12 months.

- ➤ The elderly are an ever-increasing population that will require specialized training and culturally competent care.

- ➤ Elderly clients have more co-existing physical conditions and are more likely to see their Primary Care Physicians. This indicates the need to market to the PCPs for possible referrals since our agency is trained in elder mental health care.

- ➤ Elders underutilize mental health services for a variety of reasons: inadequate insurance, shortage of trained geriatric mental health providers, lack of coordination among primary health care, stigma, and access barriers such as transportation.

- ➤ Older Americans often prefer psychotherapy to psychiatric medications.

Do you see how research can help to inform you a bit more on where to start marketing and developing your ideal client population, an avatar? It took me only ten minutes to obtain this information! The insight is well worth the time. Make sure you detail your WHY for creating your business. People will purchase from you if they can connect to you; so, be sure to figure out what your WHY is. (A sort-of mission statement.) Communicate your passion for your business. Let people know your story and why you do what you do.

6.STRATEGY & IMPLEMENTATION SUMMARY:

YGTCC will focus its marketing efforts in the following places: senior centers, local PCP offices, churches and other religious institutions, financial planners, golden sneaker programs, and the Office of Aging.

YGTCC will take Medicare, Tricare, and other major insurances that have larger populations of seniors. *(If you do not take insurance or do not want to, fantastic; each practitioner must decide for themselves if that is an option. We shall talk more about insurance later. If you are taking cash only, your places to market may be different— say, the*

Rotatory Club, golf courses (maybe a talk on how to ramp up your mind for a better golf swing?) or retirement communities.

Therapist practice in a box

Networking opportunities:

Golf courses, retirement communities, senior centers, etc. Each week one staff person will contact at least three people from this list. These meetings will focus on the needs of the community and what services YGTCC can provide. *It might be that once a week you travel to the retirement center and offer a group class. At my office, we offer a free dementia support group for caregivers once a month.* Grief, depression, and anxiety are common mental health concerns of the elderly. Therapists at YGTCC are well-versed in the Grief Recovery Model enabling them to provide excellent mental health care to those who are grieving. They are skilled in the use of other treatment modalities to provide excellent care to those who suffer from depression and/or anxiety.

The fees for services will be as follows:

Year 1 Dementia Support Group:	Free to community
Individual Therapy:	$85.00/hr.
Teenage Group Therapy:	$30.00/per client
Couples or Family Therapy:	$100.00/hr.
Victim Witness pays per session:	$83.00/hr.
Medicare pays per session:	$70.00/hr.
Average Other	$60.00/hr.
Adult Congregate Living (Elder)	$150/hr.

Year 2

In-home counseling	$ 150.00/hr.

Year 3

Teenage Group (2)	$ 40.00/session
Senior Group (2)	$40.00/session

All clinical staff are expected to see 15 clients a week and provide one group session each month.

If you are a sole practitioner, list your hours and the cost of each service; if you have more staff, list them also, for example, break out for year two and three and even five, if you are adventurous. Below is how you can break it down each year.

Therapist 1, Year 1

15 clients a week
2 family sessions @ $100.00 = $200.00
6 individual clients @ $85.00 = $510.00
2 Couples @ 100.00 =$200
3 clients @ $60.00 = $180.00
2 group sessions/monthly $30.00 x 6 clients x 2x = $360.00

Weekly Income Total: $1,450
Monthly Income Total: $5,800
Yearly Income Total (48 weeks): $69,600

Therapist practice in a box

If you are asking why I only used 48 weeks, it is because I expect, you to take some <u>vacation</u> and there will be <u>holidays</u>, client sick days, and no-shows.

Now before you jump for joy about that revenue, you must factor out the expenses.

Fixed costs per therapist/month *(You may have other costs)*:

Rent: $500.00
Phone $50 Internet: $100
Website/hosting: $100
Office supplies: $45
Biller: $25
Bookkeeper $50
Utilities: $70
Malpractice Ins.$10
General Ins. $ 15
Books and publications: $20
Taxes $ 100
Psychology Today Profile $90.00 or other 3 therapist listings **Yes, you need to have your information listed and updated often. Put it on your calendar and update with a fresh photo of you.**

Why? Because people connect with people, not just words. If you are going to trust someone with your most precious secrets, you want to see what a prospective therapist looks like.

Total Monthly Expense: $1,175
Total Monthly Profit: $4,625
Yearly Profit $55,500

These rough figures will help you plan for big expenditures and what your wages might be. Again, these are projections, but it helps map out your needs for the year. Other fixed costs might include taxes (20%), health insurance, memberships in professional organizations, networking events, training, (we all need CEUs), and maybe specialized training in specific areas, such as EMDR, DBT, etc.

Year 2

5 Therapists each performing:

4 family sessions @ $100.00 = $400.00
11 individual clients @ $85.00 = $935.00
3 couples @ 100.00 = $300
3 clients @ $60.00 = $180.00 (reduced rate or insurance clients)
2 group sessions/monthly $30.00 x 6 clients x 2= $360.00
Weekly Income Total: $2,175
Monthly Income Total: $8,700
Yearly Income Total (48 weeks): $104.400/gross Yearly
Expenses: $50,000

Yearly Profit: $54,000 X 5 therapists = $272,000/year

The services will be broadened to include more family sessions, groups and added staff for more clinical hours' total. as the expenses go up for staff or other costs, such as rent or utilities, you will need to adjust the number quarterly.

Year 3:

We plan to add five more clinicians to the staff, raising the total to 15. The added income is anticipated to be $23,125, or more, per month to the business. Now, I am not a CPA, but I do look at my numbers frequently to see if we are close to being on track. You also must be open to looking at the numbers frequently. This business plan is not one that you would use for a loan at a bank, although with some added information, it could be. It is a template of your vision of what your business can be. This plan is not hard to do, and it should only take you few hours to knock it out. I truly believe it will help set the foundation for your business. If the numbers are not what you like, or your take home is not what you like, you can now start to work on getting it where you want it.

Some people find that working backward from their expected income to what will be needed is easier. Either way, play around with the numbers. Make them your own. If they are not big enough, you can grow them, just don't give up.

Below is the basic business plan format. Be as detailed as possible and dream big, my friends. This can happen for you.

Chapter 3: The plans

Basic Business Plan Format Summary

1. Company Summary

2. Services Offered: Year 1, Year 2, Year 3

3. Business Operations

4. Market Analysis

5. Strategies and Implementation Summary

6. Fees over Three Year

Other Business Plans

You can find other FREE business plan formats from SCORE, a nonprofit that connects retired business people as mentors to new entrepreneurs to create start-up companies from this link:

http://www.scorela.org/wp-content/uploads/2012/08/Business-Plan-for-a-Startup-Business_0.doc.

Another source that is very helpful is one from Inc. Magazine link: http://www.inc.com/larry-kim/top-10-business-plan-templates-you- can-download-free.html.

Chambers of Commerce and Women's Business Centers also offer classes in business plan formats.

Tips

➤ Remember not to get hung up on the details of a plan. Do get something down on paper as a guideline of where you want to take your company. A business plan is just a good outline that helps you become organized.

➤ Know that business plans change, grow and become develop over time. Use them as a guide.

➤ Business plans can help you obtain funding, and some banks might require one to obtain a loan.

Check List of To Do Items

☐ Start to develop your niche or specialties that you enjoy working with Think about what do I want to be known.

☐ Develop your ten Frequently Asked Questions & Answers that your clients are asking about your niche and/or counseling in general.

☐ Create your avatar or ideal client: Who is the person sitting across from you? When you close your eyes, who do you picture? Write it down in as much detail as possible.

☐ Expand by creating a list of 50 things (over-achievers: 100) about your ideal client.

☐ Blogs: Write, write, and write some more!

☐ Begin preparing a Business Plan. <u>DO NOT SKIP THIS STEP!</u>

Suggested Headings:

- Company Summary
- Services Offered: Year 1, Year 2, Year 3
- Business Operations
- Market Analysis
- Strategies and Implementation Summary
- Fees over Three Years

You only fail when you stop trying. —Albert Einstein

Chapter 4: The Office

Step 1: Finding Your Spot

No doubt you have heard, "Location, location, location." It's a real estate term that means the perfect house is in the "prime spot in the community." That would include good schools, great shopping in the area, a home with a view, close to work, etc.

When applied to therapy practices, it means finding your spot; you need to ask, "Where does my ideal client live or go? Will I be in a location that they are willing and able to drive to see me?" In my city, there are a few new warehouse buildings that are easy to get to and would make great office spaces, but at the prime counseling hours, the area is very isolated, and clients could feel unsafe and fearful going there in the dark. Convenience and safety are important to clients.

As your specialty grows, clients will be willing to drive further if they really feel you can help them. I have some clients who drive 45 to 60 minutes each way weekly to attend therapy at my full fee. That is not the norm for most clients though.

Where might your ideal client be? Do want your office to be in the middle of the city or town you live in? You should be close to a university if your ideal clients are college students and close to a park or school if your ideal clients are children, families, or mothers.

We chose a location close to a shopping center in a professional building. We enjoy being near other professionals and we have the bonus of being close to high-density single-family homes, schools, churches, and easy freeway access.

Chapter 4: The office

But wait.... You also can get a location by sharing an office space with another therapist or business professional. I have a friend who found space in a doctor's office. I did not go this route because I wanted my own space to decorate and where I set the rules.

When you are just starting out this sometimes makes sense. I also had a friend that purchased an office building in Seattle for close to a million dollars; she needed a loan to obtain the building. To pay the mortgage, she rented out spaces to other professionals. Instead of paying rent for 20-25 years, she will make payments towards having something from her investment. That was a smart business decision for her.

When my business partner and I started out, we rented an office space and added a wall (at the landlord's expense) to make three rooms into four. That gave us three treatments rooms, a receptionist's spot, and waiting room. We rented out one room, and we did therapy in the other two. It worked well until the owner of the business passed away, and the new owner was not as good about maintaining the property. Plus, we wanted to expand our business by getting a larger office space. We found a newer building and negotiated the rent down to the half-cent.

Remember, everything is negotiable. If you find an office to share and you're just starting out, you might try to negotiate your rent as a percentage, for example, 20% of your income. I did this type of an arrangement with a therapist who was downsizing. Every month she paid 20% of what she made. We had set a minimum monthly rent of $400 and a maximum of $1,000. This percentage works well, especially if you and the therapist have a slow month. The minimum helps keep you on the plan.

If a shared office space is something that sounds right for you here are a few more pointers:

Therapist practice in a box

Call around in your town and see if there are any therapists or counselors, or other professionals, who have an extra room they are not using. I would ask these three discussion points:

1. In Would you be interested in a shared office agreement that could be profitable to both of us?
2. What days and times would the office be available? Often, this is weekends. (Ask yourself what will work for you.)
3. I was hoping to pay $_____ (Give an amount would that work for you.)

Here is an easy way to think through this before you have that crucial conversation. Know the fair market cost of the rent in the area or call a realtor and ask what the cost per square feet is. Once you have that number, you can negotiate the rent. If you are looking for a shared office, try asking for a flat fee, monthly cost or a percentage. Thus, if the rent is $1200 for the office, I might offer $350 -$400 a month for a flat fee amount, or you could offer a percentage of your income, say 10- 15% of what you are bringing in monthly. I have had both arrangements in my office, and both have worked well for me. Points to remember: don't lowball them; if the office space is great, a $50 to $100 savings may not be worth it. Furthermore, the relationship you develop could also be a referral source once they get to know and trust you. Think a little about this. If one client earns you $2,500.00 a year, then a few good referrals and your income will far offset the cost of monthly rent.Be honest, when you are first starting, tell them you have no clients yet. Ask if they would be kind enough to give you a break while you are building up the practice. Ask for six months and tell them you will give them an increase after that. Plus, if they don't feel it's a good fit for them after six months, you will leave— no harm, no foul. The amount of rent may sound a little scary at first, and it is, but once you start seeing clients, paying the rent becomes easier and easier, and it will not be as scary.

The Basic Contract

Some therapist "landlords" charge rent by the hour, day, or take 10% of every client seen. I only charge per month for the room, so I can't advise shorter times. A month can be broken down into part/full time. {Whatever way you do it, please, PLEASE, PLEASE, *get it in writing.*

The basic contract would include:

- Hours: Usage? Is your room being used when you not there? Is it available nights, weekends, holidays?
- Clean up: Who takes out the trash?
- Rent: How is it calculated, percent, or flat fee? What is the due date? If it's late, what is the fee?
- Parking: Availability? A number of spaces?
- Other considerations: What's included – a kitchen, phone, costs for keys, onsite storage for files, restrooms, heat and A/C?

We almost rented a building that had no air conditioning during the weekend. It was part of a bank building with one master air conditioning unit. If we wanted to use the A/C when the bank was closed, it would cost $150 per day. Needless to say, we did not go with that building.

The contract will save you and the professional that rents to you a great deal of time, aggravation, money, and hurt feelings. A commercial landlord will insist on a contract, but therapists or other professionals who are sometimes subletting do not insist on a contract. Having one avoids the "I thought it would be like" or "I assumed he would let me work on Saturdays, but the office is not open." Not having a contact can make for stressful relationships and unintended problems. Do the right thing and request or create that contract and be specific as to what are your rights and responsibilities.

Out of Your Home?

Lastly, I want to give you one more possible alternative to owning or renting your space. I have at least four therapist friends who run their therapy business out of their home. That was not an option for me, as my home's floor plan does not accommodate a separate business space. My friends each have homes that accommodate "the office" setting easily and having this works wonderfully for them. Plus, their commute time only takes them a minute to walk to work. If you are thinking about your home your office space, there are **special considerations** to think about. To run a successful therapy business from your home office:

1. You must carefully screen the clients as they will be coming to your home.

2. Think about your space and the specific niches you work with. If you see children, do you have room for play therapy and toys?

3. Can you see couples and children back to back, or do you have children one day with toys and couples another day? Watch your flow.

4. Spell out your "informed consent." Be clear that the client cannot just stop by like they can with other

businesses. They must have and keep their scheduled appointments.

5. All clients should be nonviolent and have no criminal history.

6. Trust your own gut for safety. If at any time something doesn't feel right, do not take on a client.

7. At times, this arrangement may not work for clients as they feel too uncomfortable to go to their therapist's home.

8. Network with other home-office therapists for a tribe and support. You can find a Facebook group of over 100 at- home therapists that are having good discussions on this topic.

Other Points to Consider

- What other businesses are in the area and in your specific building

- Visit the space at different days and times than when you would normally be in the office. Is the neighborhood safe for you and your client? Now go off hours, say a client needs an emergency appointment or you're doing billing, still feel safe?

- How will you create a warm and inviting office?

- How will you handle the phones? The biggest reason therapists do not get appointments is their phone is not answered consistently, or they do not return calls. You do not need to hire full-time staff or do this all by yourself. You might use a phone answering service, a virtual assistant (VA), a practice manager, etc. If you are answering all calls, make sure to check your phone often and leave time to return calls during the day. Do not wait until the end of the day when you are tired and ready to go home. In our business, we have used retired seniors, college students, our adult children, and hired staff to answer phones. We just make sure the phone calls get returned promptly.

- Always try to add value to a client interaction. It really will pay off. Please do not be that therapist who doesn't return calls or answer the phone. Always call back, hear their pain and respond in a positive manner. Make referrals if the clients are not your ideal client.

- Your office will need the internet and a phone system. Look around and see what is reliable and cost-effective. We went with a landline for the main office phone and FAX. We use cell phones for the therapists and our off-site VA who answers our phones when we are all in session and when our reception staff is unavailable.

- My friend, the Fire Marshall, would be upset if I didn't mention having at least one ABC-type fire extinguisher in your office. When you get your city business license, your business is added to the Fire Marshall's list. Our first office had fire extinguishers in each office suite, and the landlord maintained them. In our new office suite, that is not the case, and it is now a new responsibility to make sure we have extinguishers. This is an out of sight/out of mind item. However, I would argue that they are as important as the pens, paper, and the internet for your office.

- While we are on the important topic of safety, I would also ask that you invest in a small first aid kit. We do not use ours very often, but every once in a while, we have a papercut, staple puncture, or minor accident. Band-Aid™ plastic strips and other items have been used. The Girl Scout's motto, "Be Prepared," is still a good sentiment in today's business world.

- We also installed a security camera and save a month's worth of video to the cloud. We have this camera for overall safety. We can access the camera from our computer or smartphone. At times, we have played back interactions between people in the waiting room especially when one person's behavior has not been appropriate. One of my colleagues who does divorce, and mediation said that at times watching the interaction between her family members is invaluable. Personally, I am not watching clients; I just like being able to see the front door if I am alone in my office in the evening. If you are a sole practitioner, this item might be invaluable to you too. The camera is easy to install; ours is a simple plug-and-play. Bottom line: think SAFETY always. Also, we do have a sign in the office informing people that a video is in progress and the cameras are in plain sight. Additionally, we have it listed in our office policies to notify each client of our security purposes.

Step 2: Basic Office Equipment

If you are starting with an empty room, you will need to create a functional office space, which requires some basic office equipment. Here are the basics.

- Land Line and Cell Telephones

We have both a landline and a cell phone. We chose a landline for the 911 safety factor, as it goes directly to the local police station. A cell phone goes to the Highway Patrol, and they transfer the call to the local police or fire station. That takes more time, and we wanted to have a direct link. By having a landline, we have had fewer dropped calls and clearer sound quality. It also lists us for FREE in the White Pages Directory. Most paper directories have gone away, they have been replaced with online ones. While we are listed in directories, do not pay for the Yellow Pages or any other for that matter. That is an expense you do not need. We also use a cell phone as one of our lines into our business. I know that with VOIP (Voice Over the Internet) the sound quality has improved since the broadband connections have gotten faster and more powerful. We know that many of our clients prefer to text us, so by having a cell phone option we can receive direct text messages. When we ran a Google Ad campaign, we had both a phone number and text number listed and received at least 50% of our replies via text messages. We have since discontinued that ad, but we still get inquiries via text daily. The questions we are getting range from whether we are accepting new clients or asking for directions to clients letting us know they are running late. We are a mobile society and clients embrace new technologies; therapists and counselors must as well.

- A Cell Phone Only

If you want to use a cell phone *only,* you can easily make that work too. A cell phone may cost you a lot less in the long run. For safety's sake, however, pre-program the direct numbers of the local fire and police stations into your cell phone to save you time and create a better safety net for your practice. A couple of programs that may help you decide are Grasshopper.com and Phone.com. These have many features that allow small businesses to have the features of big corporations. These two companies are similar; they allow clients to call in and use a directory to reach their therapist. You can have one of your extensions give your address and directions.

Thus, eliminating you or office staff from taking those calls. In my office, we have a VA (a live person not at our office) answer the new client line and schedule appointments for the 12 therapists. Further, each therapist has their own personal voicemail. Because we are mobility connected, the use of these services can also allow the therapist to use a personal cell to return calls, but the number on the caller ID shows up with our office number, thus, protecting the therapist's personal cell phone number from the client. Having this system gives my therapists the flexibility returning phone calls away from the office, having to own only one phone and protecting privacy. Win-win.

- Desks and Comfortable Chairs

We spend so much time at sitting at our desk or while in session; it is important to have a functional and comfortable chair. I would have you consider a standing desk as we tend to sit a lot, and a standing desk is a nice way to stretch and get the blood moving. Sitting too much seems to be the new smoking in terms of being bad for our health. If you can't afford one at least stand up while making and returning phone calls and pace while talking; it will open your mind and get the blood flowing in your brain.

- Locking File Cabinet

This is for all paper documentation that has client identifying information or Protected Health Information (PHI). Even with the use of an Electronic Medical Record (EMR), you will still have a few paper documents.

- Copier, Printer and Fax Machine

We use an all-in-one machine. It's built for business, so it is a bit sturdier than the models for home use. We use a dedicated FAX number in a locked room rather than use the local FAX services of FedEx-Kinkos or Staples. It's more secure, more convenient and allows you to receive Explanation of Benefits (EOB), requests from State Disabilities and Victims of Crime, and the like. If you are using a public FAX, PHI could be compromised. There are other FAX services, but you must be careful to comply with all HIPAA regulations. (Faxage.com is one such service.) If you are a HIPAA secure entity, choose carefully. There are also applications for smartphones, and I am sure, there will be other HIPAA options in the future as technology continues to develop.

- <u>Comfortable Furniture for Your Clients</u>

Make sure you find comfortable, professional-looking furniture for your office and waiting room. Your chair or couch will endure a lot of sitting, and you need good support for you and your clients. Furniture is expensive, and if you're just starting out, hand-me-downs can mean big savings. Just make sure that they are not worn or ragged and that they go with the vibe you're trying to create. When we were setting up our first office, we were lucky enough to find a few newish, high-end office chairs that the previous owner did not use much. They looked great and matched our overall theme, at about half the cost of brand new chairs.

- <u>Computer</u>

A computer is pretty much standard equipment these days. I would suggest a new computer if possible and have it dedicated only for your work. It's not a good idea for others to use the work computer, it contains sensitive material like client letters, reports or client records. It is better to keep personal and work life separate. I encourage you to install great antivirus and malware protection, and always have the computer password protected.

- <u>Office Supplies</u>

Paper, pens, pencils, tape, staples, staplers, paper clips, trash cans, and the like are basic items. I also have a whiteboard and a bulletin board I use in my office. My office team also uses portable whiteboards to help diagram themes for a clients' goals. The client can take a photo of the board and refer to it during the week. On the waiting room bulletin board, we post groups, resources, quotes, and other information we want our clients to know. We buy a ton of office supplies at the back-to-school sales each year.

- <u>Water Bottle or Personal Cup</u>

I know a water bottle or personal cup that you love is not traditional office equipment. This is really for self-care, but it's super important to stay hydrated. I love my stainless-steel bottle that keeps both my hot and cold liquids at the perfect temperature. Aim for at least two liters, 68 ounces, of water daily. This is very important. Water will help your brain as you process all this new stuff.

TIP: Create an account with Amazon or Staples both have good prices on many of these things you will use in your office, and they deliver. That alone will help save you time to work on your business.

Check List of To Do Items

☐ *Find a good location for your business.*

☐ *Review pros and cons of location& cost. Take your time; leases last a few years, so plan carefully.*

☐ *If using a shared office arrangement get a contract in writing.*

☐ *Start collecting basic office equipment. What do you have access to?*

• *What do you need?*

☐ *Create your paperwork; start preparing your forms. Think about office policies, informed consents, intakes, etc.*

☐ *How's the self-care coming along? Make sure you are taking time this is an on-going action item*

"Paperwork wouldn't be so bad if it weren't for all the paper. And the work."
— Darynda Jones

Chapter 5: Sorting Out the Paperwork

Step 1: Electronic records or paper?

Whether to go for electronic record keeping (EMR) or paper is an important consideration. When I was starting out, electronic record keeping was only for big practices, and the programs were clunky and hard to manage. We tried a few and just couldn't get the hang of it. We went with old-fashioned paper records. We created our forms, then had them reviewed by the association we belonged to, and ran them past every clinician we knew to see if they were easy and workable. We pulled together all the proper documents, and we were off. I review the forms yearly by setting up an on-going calendar date to review and update my forms. This is important because as you figure out your goals and what is working well and what is not, you will have the time already set aside to create updates to your forms. Make sure all the current information and new laws have been addressed in the revisions yearly. Remember paper forms require you to invest in locking file cabinets.

If you decide to go electronic, I am happy to report there are a number of good programs out there. Currently, we are using a program called TheraNest. They have a great price for a group practice, and they are easy to use and set up. Our therapists transitioned to this system without much trouble. Other programs include Simple Practice (written by a therapist), TheraNote, and Practice Ally. We decided to upgrade to electronic record keeping to better keep track of files— once we had 10 to 12 therapists in my group, it became darn near impossible to keep track of the paper files. We have found that using an EMR system has many positives, including less paper (in fact, a *lot* less paper, which is better for the environment and saves money). Plus, it is easy to review notes of other therapists, associates and interns.

Step 2: Forms you need to START...

Please note there may be specific forms you need if you are outside California. Make sure to check with your professional organization and licensing board. These are the forms we use daily:

1. **Client Information:** (registration) This form has client demographics and the necessary information to bill insurance. We also collect referral sources, email addresses, and who to contact in case of an emergency (think Tarasoff v Regents of the University of California "Duty to Warn"' and Ewing v. Goldstein. The court expanded the definition of Civil Code § 43.92 to "include family members can provide information to the therapist." (California, 2004)

2. **Informed consent:**

   a. Special informed consents, i.e., child custody services, coaching, children 12 and up, a group participation form should be used and not the standardized form.
   b. General office consents, (look at what is required in your state).

3. **Fees statement**: Clearly spell out what you charge for each service. Be clear and include items like letter writing, additional phone calls between sessions, court costs, etc. These can be part of your informed consent or a separate document.

4. **Missed appointments policy**: Think about your time, set a boundary and stick to it.

5. **Credit card**: A form to store credit card information. This gives you the ability to charge for copays, session fees, or missed appointments fees; this is a must.

6. **Office policies**: This should include things like confidentiality and exceptions, hours, emergency contacts, and cancellation time frames. This form could be separate or part of the informed consent.

7. **Social Media Policy:** We spell out our policy about not following our clients or friending them, or even asking them to rate our service.

8. **Assessments:** Intake forms/social history, presenting problems and symptoms, mental status, drugs, alcohol suicidality/homicidally, genogram, etc., (this used during the initial intake interview).

9. **Progress Notes**: The weekly note or contact we have with each client. Don't forget to document every phone call, case consult, and all supervision contacts or staffing of this case with a supervisor or colleagues.

10. **The release of Information:** We have our clients sign a release for us to speak to other professionals, such as

the primary care physician, psychiatrist, past therapist, lawyer, social workers, etc. If clients want us to write a letter for anything on their behalf, we have them sign a release form. We will also have them sign a release to speak to specific people at their insurance company. Better safe than sorry.

11. **(BONUS) Notice of Information (HIPAA):** Spell out to your clients what you are doing to protect their privacy.

12. **(Optional) Welcome Letter:** We use this to introduce ourselves and our practice. Since we are the owners of this group we want to provide superior service, but we also want our clients to know we care, and give them an easy way to contact us. I provide my cell number and ask that the client call me if they have any concern or problems with our office, staff or their therapeutic plan. We want them to be happy as possible with the process. In seven years, we have had only two clients change therapists due to "just not a good fit." Since I started providing my personal cell number, I have only received one call after hours. I think a Welcome Letter is part of what sets us apart from the crowd.

TIP: Automate sending these forms out if possible. We have our forms on our client portal within our EMR; there the client can fill out the paperwork before their intake session. When it's filled out online, it automatically becomes part of our clinical record and is saved in their file. If you cannot afford an EMR, then the next best idea would be to create your intake forms as fillable PDF files and email the client the forms. This step will save you time and money by not having to print all your forms over and over. I suggest having a few extra copies in the office, just in case.

You can even create an electronic signature allowing your clients to sign paperwork and return it to you via email, again saving time and money. Be sure to list in your paperwork the phrase "Acceptance of the electronic signature constitutes as a true and correct signature." Electronic signatures are becoming commonplace, but it is our duty to go the extra mile in disclosures for our clients. Electronic or PDF files can easily completed by you, or it can be outsourced to a VA at a reasonable cost. You can find VA for this on Fiverr.com or Upwork.com or ask other therapists. Creating PDF intake files, it makes the file small enough to easily email them to your clients.

I have the above packet on my website: www.therapistbox.com; enter the promotion code **20 percent**. These are ready for immediate download.

Step 3: Guidance for Logos

First and foremost, make sure you love it. I mean really, really love it. You will use it on everything from signage to print ads, social media, and business cards. You want to brand yourself, so use it everywhere you can think of.

Look for color combinations that evoke positive feelings. Some therapists are using initials for a logo, or a symbol as their company's name. Do not use too many colors, as that can get costly to reproduce and may not look good in black and white if needed for some printed signs. For instance, in my building, you can only have white letters on the actual door. If you use a lot of colors, it may lose the logo when printed monochrome. Use the world as inspiration: look around and see what colors and shapes catch your eye. Don't make your logo too busy or hard to read with tiny print. Ask yourself, "What am I trying to convey?"

Good color choice is particularly important. Jeff Haden, a contributing editor at Inc. Magazine, created a cool graphic that can be seen at http://on.inc.com/1rKBB1a. I have summarized the colors below:

- Red: intensity, active, fire, passion, trust, love, aggressiveness
- Blue: professional, faith, understanding, comfort
- Yellow: joy, love, fresh, energetic
- Green: growth, calm, trust, peaceful, hopeful, nature
- Purple: royalty, luxury, power, glamor, romantic
- Orange: happiness, determined, creative, enthusiastic
- Pink: feminine, warm, sweet, nurtured, sexuality
- Brown: dependability, mother nature, support, reliability

As you think about your logo and branding, think about what emotions you are trying to invoke. Your logo must resonate with you and who you are. Take your time with this one. It is important.

Where do you look for logos?

Start by looking at Google images. What do you like? What catches your eye? Companies like 99 Designs, Logo Generators, and Fiverr all have the ability to create logos for you at a reasonable cost. I have had a few logos for my business. My first one was generated by a talented graphic artist. Our second one came from 99 Designs, and my last four came from graphic artists on Fiverr.

Fun trivia fact: Coke-A-Cola, Microsoft, and Google original logos were designed for free by the owner or an employee of the company. The Twitter bird symbol cost only $15.00 with only $6.00 going to the artist.

When you have an artist create a logo for you ask that they provide you with a few different file types. It will cost you more upfront, but trust me it will be well worth it over the years. When you market your practice, you will need different files for specific projects. For example, for large signs, banners or tablecloths you will need a larger file format. If you use PDF or Jpeg files when enlarged these files will create distorted pictures of your logo. But if you have an .ai or .eps file, they can be enlarged and not lose picture quality. You would not want your logo pixelating (breaking apart). Other files you will also need are the reverse color logo and a transparent logo file for printing. Also, ask for a compressed file that can be used on websites to increase the loading speeds. Additionally, ask your designer what the color code numbers are for your logos. They should be able to provide you either the Hex code or the RBG (red, blue, green) codes.

Hex codes and RGBs are mathematical computations for color, which in printing is separated into red, green, and blue. Without getting into the weeds, all you need to know are the numbers for the colors in your logos and brands to stay consistent on all products and social media posts. Hex codes are expressed as the symbol # followed by a combination of six number and letters. The combination of the code breaks the colors down as # XX(red) XX(Green) XX(Blue). For example,

Black is the absence of color, so its Hex code is #000000, Red is #FF0000 (primary), Yellow is # FFFF0O (primary).

RGB stands for the percentage of red, green and blue within the final color. RGB is represented as RGB 0,0,0 (black), RGB 255,0,0 (red) or RGB 255,255,0 (yellow). See all the color codes or convert from Hex to RGB or vice versa at this link. http://htmlcolorcodes.com/.

File Extensions

Your logo files should have different extensions, for example mylogo.ai or mylogo.jpeg (Look for the dot[.] and two or three letter extensions). The common ones you will need for different projects:

.AI are Illustrator files created in the Adobe Illustrator program; they are native vector files or sometimes called source files. You most likely will not have Adobe Illustrator on your computer; that is okay. You still will need at least one of these files of your logo. This type of file can be used by graphic designers to create promotional items big or small without looking muddy or pixelating your logo. You could use the large format for an outdoor sign for the office building or a small version of the same file for a pencil. Both items would look great coming from this type of file. You may never be able to open the file in this format but the professionals that create these products will. This type of file is a must.

.EPS (Encapsulated PostScript) files are a vector format of your logo. A vector file is highly versatile, allowing you to resize your logo without losing clarity and print quality. .EPS files are created in many professional drawing programs including Adobe Illustrator. This type of file is the gold standard of files, as it will never compromise the quality of the logo as you resize it.

Therapist practice in a box

Suitable uses for this file include advertisements, brochures, and business cards.

.PDF is a common file type that can be opened in Adobe Acrobat Reader or another common reader. This type of vector file can be opened and modified by the non-professional and can be viewed on most computers, smartphones, or tablets. It can be resized and manipulated for different types of print work. This is an easy file to work in and in a pinch, can be used by a professional as a source file if you do not have a .ai file. Bottom line: this is a must have file.

.PS stands for PhotoShop™ files. This is a source file, but unless you have Adobe PhotoShop™, you will never use it. It is useful for large print items. If you have a .ai or a .EPS, you don't need this file. But if you have it, save it as it may come in handy for the professional helping you at some point.

.JPG,PNG,GIF, TIF, and .BMP files are pixel-type files. These are used on websites, social media, or TV screens. You can make the image smaller without losing quality but never bigger. They are hard to resize and sometimes can't be at all. Sometimes these types of files are called "fixed media" files.

.JPG or you may see it as written as **JPEG**. That stands for Joint Photographic Expert Group. This is a small file size, can be compressed, and has a background. JPG load quickly on internet pages. You need to get a few different sizes. These files come from digital cameras.

.PNG files are slightly larger, and the main advantage is they can have a transparent background so that they can be overlaid on background colors. If your logo has color blends or gradients this the format, you want.

Chapter 5: Sorting out the paperwork

.GIF file format is older and has a limited color range. I would skip this file type.

.TIF and.**BMP** files are high-quality pixel files that can be used for high-quality screen files such as social media or websites. These can be modified. They are larger files and take up more space on your hard drive.

There is just one more file type I want to discuss: is a **SVG** file or Scalable Vector Graphic file. This is a relatively new type of hybrid file that is smaller and can be modified. They are not widely used yet, but if your designer offers you one for free or at a reasonable cost, take it.

Regardless of what file types you use, always remember to ask for the RBG and Hex codes so that any future graphics are consistent with your brand colors.

The bottom line needed files for logo files or any graphic files you have created:

- AI (Wonderful to have but you won't use this one, only professional artists will, But you do need this If you want clear logos on pens or banners this is absolute must)

- EPS (MUST)

- PDF (MUST)

- JPG/JPEG (Get a couple of sizes)

- PNG (Get a couple of sizes)

Step 4: Business Cards

Once you have your physical location and a logo, it's time to order business cards! Keep branding in mind, using the colors that coordinate with your website and paperwork such as stationery and forms. Some printers we have used include Vista Print, Moo, and GotPrint.com. The front side of our card has the traditional items: name, title, address, phone, fax, email, and website. On the back side of our cards, we have our logo and the next appointment date. By using our business cards as our next appointment card, it's become a convenient way for the client to remember their appointment and find the phone number easily to reschedule if needed. Don't waste your money on glossy finishes or photo paper; they are difficult to write on and cost twice as much. When I network with other professionals, we exchange business cards; I usually jot down a few details on each card. It helps me remember the person I was networking with. Also, if I have agreed to send them something like one of my articles or introduction to another professional, I write it on the card. If the card is shiny, it's hard to do with a regular pen.

Additional Pointers:

- Make sure the font is large enough to be easily read. You may have 20/20 vision, but many clients do not.

- Use strong contrasts; it's hard to read light colors on light backgrounds.

- Coordinate with your website colors.

Chapter 5: Sorting out the paperwork

- Email and company website addresses are a must.

- Keep business cards in a business card holder, not in your wallet. No one wants that bent card.

- Provide multiple cards to friends, family, and others who can distribute them to other possible referral sources such as doctors, lawyers, teachers, etc.

- Some therapists include their social media contacts. I don't, but I am thinking about it. It's your call, how connected you want to be with clients and prospective clients.

- Here is another idea I have seen from a few companies. The front of the card has the expected contact information. On the back, instead of the blank card or the appointment time, some have cool sayings on the back. A furniture company where we purchased stuff for the office had these great cards. On the back, they had sayings like "Choose Happy," "Everyone makes mistakes; learn from it.", "Don't give up.", "Love never leaves, but people do." I like this idea, but we chose not to have the additional cost during our startup. It may be an idea we revisit. I have also recently heard of other therapists expanding on this idea.

- We include a tasteful reminder about our 24-hour cancellation policy on the back.

Step 5: Organize the Receipts

Now that you're in business save ALL receipts! When you begin to purchase items for your business, you will need receipts for your accountant and the tax record. Create a place to keep all your receipts safe and organized. I keep my monthly receipts in a large envelope. At the end of the year, I compile all the months into one large envelope. I know some therapists scan the receipts into a file folder. For me, that is too much work. All my purchases go into my QuickBooks online system. It learns my categories and does most of the work. The physical receipts will be needed for your accountant or if you are ever called to a tax audit. I put them in categories as I collect them over the months: credit cards, electric bill, rent, etc. This system works well for me. Find what works best for you, but definitely create a system that you will use.

Additional pointers

- Keep all paperwork for your business (I use a notebook for the paper I must save)
    - IRS SS-4
    - Fictitious Name Statement
    - Receipts for all business purchases
    - Business plan
    - Fire permits

- Organize all your important numbers and data in one place; I use an old-school notebook to list all these. The notebook is easily pulled out when I need some information. This will help with insurance credentialing if needed, and will also make tax preparation easier

●

The list below is a good start:

- ○ EIN Tax ID (Try to memorize this number because you will use it a lot!)
- ○ NPI number.
- ○ License number and expiration date; some insurance companies want first issuance date also.
- ○ Date of birth for you and your staff
- ○ Specialized training. W-9, the tax form you provide to those who pay you, such as insurance companies, agencies you do contract work for, i.e., speaking engagements, supervising interns, etc.
- ○ Domain names & passwords consider a Password Manager. I really recommend this.

Check List of To Do Items

☐ *Find a good location for your business.*

☐ *Review pros and cons of location& cost. Take your time; leases last a few years, so plan carefully.*

☐ *Start collecting basic office equipment. What do you have access to?*

☐ *What do you need?*

☐ *Paperwork; start preparing your forms. Think about office policies, informed consents, intakes, etc.*

☐ *Electronic records vs. paper records?*

☐ *Logo Design, start thinking about how you want to represent your business.*

☐ *File Extensions; make sure you have the proper ones.*

☐ *Design business cards and have them printed.*

☐ *Create a file for all receipts; label clearly.*

☐ *When was the last time you had a bit of fun? Go play, enjoy your family, smile and laugh!*

"What would you do if you weren't afraid?"

— *Sheryl Sandberg,*

Chapter 6: The Numbers

Step 1: It's Banking Time!

No matter what type of business structure you select, you *must* have business checking and savings accounts. *Never* co-mingle personal and business funds; that is an easy way to get into a lot of trouble.

Yes, I know you're not making money yet, but you *will* so set up that savings account now. When you make your first deposit (from personal funds), write yourself a receipt with the amount, date, and purpose - Startup Capital Loan, (you are saving all receipts, right?) This is an important one that you will need later. Now you have your first liability, and at some point, you will pay yourself (personal) back for that loan (business).

Research banks, credit unions, savings and loans, and find one with free business accounts. Don't spend a lot of money on adding a logo to your business checks. It's not worth it, in most cases, you will probably pay your bills online. However, you will need checks occasionally. My current landlord doesn't accept direct deposits. I don't understand it, but he is a bit old-fashioned that way.

Once you've chosen a bank, you will need your IRS Form SS-4 to prove your business structure and the legal name you are using. If you are a partnership or corporation, you may need your letters of incorporation and/or minutes stating who are the officers if your business. Only officers and/or owners should have access to the bank's accounts and ATM cards. You will also need a photo ID, and some banks require a copy of your business license. Call ahead to see what your bank requires.

My free business account came with a line of credit and a credit card. While these are not 100% necessary, sometimes they can help when cash flow is low. A few years back when we hired a few therapists, we estimated the costs, including employment taxes which you should figure at about 25%. We knew how much work they had to complete and how much we would be receiving. Then we were hit by a perfect storm; our biller was out sick for a week and a half, during which time our mailboxes were broken into, the post office was holding our mail due to the broken box, and of course it was after 5 pm, the post office was closed, and payroll was due! I looked at the bank balances and knew we didn't have enough to cover the expenses. Because we had that line of credit, I was able to transfer $5000.00 for payroll into the checking account. The following Monday, I went to the post office, picked up a few checks, and made a deposit. My biller followed up on two checks that were stolen and sent the requests to the payers to stop the checks and reissue our payment. By Friday of the next week, I had happy therapists who received their checks on time.

Don't use a line of credit for things you can wait for or don't need—like fancy stationery or computers. Save it for emergencies.

Step 2: Taxes, Let's Prepare

Since we just spoke about banking, it's a good idea to talk about how to prepare to file business taxes. For the first couple of years, you may not owe taxes because of all the startup costs that you will be able to write off. You may owe self-employment taxes, so please keep in mind that you will pay taxes at some point in your business, and it's better to prepare. Plan that about 25-30% of all your income will go to taxes. It can vary, and only your accountant or CPA can tell you the exact number. That may seem like a big bite from your profits, but once you take out Federal and State taxes, Medicaid, SDI, and Social Security, it really adds up. When you own your business, you have all these self-employment taxes to pay, and it's better to be prepared and to get in the proper mindset, by saving the money you need for taxes.

I had a dentist friend who didn't save for his taxes. In fact, he put that 30% down on a soon to be regretted sports car. That first year he owed $12,000, the amount he put down for his new car. For him to pay the IRS, he had to borrow money at 7% to cover the taxes he owed. In the end, he had a tax bill, a car loan, and a new 7% credit card bill. Don't be that guy. Please remember to put that money into your savings account for tax time.

Step 3: Accounting Software

As a business owner, you must treat your business like the adult it is, and you must develop accounting procedures. Accounting software can be a great help, and there are many different programs to choose from. The free ones are (or were at the time of this writing): www.mint.com are www.waveaccounting.com. Other accounting software that some of my therapist friends use are www.Xero.com and www.Zohobooks.com.

Under the heading of "not free," QuickBooks is a standard in the field, and it is what my accountant asked me to use. For me, it was initially hard to learn. I am not an accountant, nor have I ever dreamed of being one. However, I bit the bullet and went this route. I used the online training classes, and they help, but there was a learning curve. This type of program, you see, is robust and can do many different actions. I purchased my first QuickBooks software package through Costco for around $175.00 bucks. I used the professional version for about four years. I had a computer crash, and fortunately, I had been religious about keeping backup copies. *Please* make sure you regularly update your backup copies! We only lost seven days' worth of records, but that was still quite a bit. When I was looking to update to the current version, I decided to try Online QuickBooks. There is a monthly subscription (which I was not 100% thrilled with), but I tried the trial version and found it was easier to use and my bookkeeper can access it from her office. I was also able to get the monthly fee reduced by going through the Costco link. Bless Costco! This online version is perfect for my business, and my bookkeeper is pleased when tax time rolls around. This program integrates well with the banking accounts and credit cards, as it automatically uploads transactions. It then sends you emails to let you know *"everything is great, carry on,"* or that you need to look at specific transitions. I would strongly suggest that, unless you are very small business, have an accounting background, or have run another small business, you really should consider getting a bookkeeper, accountant, or a CPA on your team to answer questions. I do not use my CPA more than a couple of times a year, but he is well worth his fee when I need him. My bookkeeper handles the day-to-day and monthly accounting for me. This is an investment you really should consider.

Step 4: Staying Focused on Building Your Practice

When you are first starting, schedule time to work specifically on your business. Put your phone in airplane mode, turn off notifications, and do not open any email. Start to think about email as other people's goals and desires and not yours; frankly, it can wait. You must use your time wisely and decrease as many distractions as possible. Many of us experience the occasional bout of FOMO (Fear of Missing Out syndrome) when we let ourselves get distracted by Facebook, Instagram, or anything that others are doing. We get caught up thinking, "Oh, look what they are doing! I wonder if I should do that?" We become anxious or distracted by events or activities that are happening everywhere else, and when we become distracted, we lose our focus.

Another phenomenon is SOS (Shiny Object Syndrome), defined as anything that grabs our attention or things that we become attracted to.

Both of these syndromes will sneak up on you before you know it and you'll lose precious hours. Think about checking Facebook, for instance. "Just one look" turns into half an hour and we don't even know how that happened. We all have had these distractions sometime in our life. However, if you want the freedom of owning your own practice, you must have the discipline to create the dedicated and consistent time to build your business. For those who are always in touch electronically, it may be hard to shut out the world for a short time, but it is worth it. Here are some apps that can help you manage your time if you get distracted easily:

- Focus Booster: (Mac or Windows) Breaks downtime on projects into 25 minutes "Pomodoro's." Based on the

Pomodoro's Technique: high-intensity work broken down into a block of time. Google it.

- Focus Writer: (Mac or Windows) turns your writing screen into a distraction-free zone.

- Rescue Time: (Apple/Android) helps you determine where you are spending your time and can help set goals and eliminate distractions

- Sound Curtin: (Apple) or White Noise (Android) mobile apps help block out outside noise while you are, say working on your website at Starbucks. Think white noise machine; be sure to have your earbuds.

Step 5: Setting Your Fee

It's time to talk about setting your fee and, ultimately, knowing your own worth. If you accept insurance, you will be paid a contract amount. It could be $100.00, $75.00, or even $50.00 per session. The contract you sign will tell you what you are making, which is why you MUST read contracts carefully. Even so, sometimes it is still not clear, as the contract may say something like "fees will be paid in accordance to state and federal Medical and Medicare billing." I still have no idea what that means or where I would look to find out. So, you will need to call the company to clarify before signing their contract. Once you have the information, you can determine If the fee is too low or reasonable. I recommend that if the fee is too low, walk away.

You will find clients that can pay or have higher insurance allowances. I know it's easy for me to say that since you are about to start building a practice and probably feel that any money is good money. But honestly you may come to resent those insurance clients, and you can use that time better to promote your business at the rate you want. With my crisis work, which often requires that I travel to the crisis site the insurance company negotiated a rate with me. I knew the amount I needed to have to compel me to leave my office, and I also wanted to be paid for travel time. At first, they said, "No, we do not pay that high." I replied, "That's okay. I don't have to work for you." I was prepared to walk away; I really was. Then they said, "Well wait, I will talk to my supervisor." Not only did I make what I would have made if I were in my office, but I also received payment for my travel time.

I do not use a sliding, income-based scale for clients. We have a hybrid, in that we take a limited amount of insurance and cash pay. We do not use sliding scales because we take insurance. We consider that is our sliding scale because most insurance companies pay so much less than our actual worth. Insurance companies get away with paying less in fees because they say they will refer lots of clients. They also say that because the client sees the therapist so often, the fee must be reduced. It has been our experience that insurance companies do not refer a great number of our clients, but many of our clients like to use their insurance for services. Further, we have many clients who pay our cash rates, and we further our income stream by doing some work that is not covered by insurance, such as adoption assessments, co-parenting classes, teaching, and couples work.

When you are beginning, an easy way to set a fee is to think about how much money you want to make in a year. If you want to make $80,000/year gross (before expenses), you would need to make $6,666 a month gross. If that is not enough money— and it may not be—adjust the total yearly amount.

Chapter 6: The numbers

Here's how it works. Divide your yearly goal amount by how many weeks you want to work. I recommend no more than 48 weeks. Think vacation, sick time, holidays, a day to play with your spouse or kids, conferences, all work days with no income. In my example, you divide by 48 weeks; that would mean you would need to make $1,666.66 a week. Then divide that by days worked— in my case 5 — and that works out to $333.33 a day. Now, here is the cool part. If you are making a $100.00/per client, you would need to see three and 1/3 clients a day. So, if you see four clients a day, you earn $400.00 per day. That gives you the opportunity to build in a cushion for unforeseen circumstances, no-show clients, heavy snow or rain days, or in my part of the world the A/C goes out, and your office temperature is over 110 degrees (not conducive to the therapeutic process!). So, you see how you can play with the numbers to make them work for you. If you add the insurance rate of pay and how many clients you will see at that rate, it will give you the number of additional clients you need.

The formula looks like this:

Total Yearly Gross Income	$_____
Divided by the # of weeks worked	(XX) _____ =
Divided by days worked	(X)_____ =
Divided by # of sessions a day	$_____per/client

General Suggestions

- Consider your personal energy level, carefully and honestly. Can you see more than four or six clients in a day? Think long term. Can you maintain this type of schedule?

- Maybe you can see seven clients a day, but you don't want to work five days a week. Maybe you see seven clients on two days, separated by a day (to catch up on notes, bookkeeping, working on a side hustle, etc.) then see six clients for a total of twenty clients a week. Twenty clients a week at $100.00 a session would give you $2,000 a week, well above your weekly goal in the above example.

- Want to create a therapy group and leverage your time? Running groups can be lucrative if you get the numbers for a group. Please be aware that insurance companies do not reimburse at the same rates for groups as they do for individuals. Check with each insurance company beforehand, as some insurance companies require pre-authorization before paying for groups. some types of groups, such as co-parenting or creativity workshops, are not covered by insurance, but that's okay if you can get a good-sized group together who are willing to pay out of pocket for your services. For example, our co-parenting group, which helps newly divorced couples navigate how to raise their child successfully in two homes, is structured in two-hour blocks for four weeks and we offer it six times a year. It is almost always full, and the participants must pay out of pocket for the classes. To start a group, you should start out with at least eight to ten participants. That way you will not have much of a loss when one or two do not show each week. In our very first Co-parenting group, we had only two couples. It may take a while to build up a reputation and get the word out, so be patient. Other successful groups we have run include a creativity group, teen groups, transgender support groups, and a kid's socialization group. What type of group would you like to run? Think back to your ideal clients and what they need. Here is the math on our group. A co-parenting group is a cash-only group. We charge $250.00 per person, and we have on average six people. That equals $1500.00 total. The group runs four sessions for a total of eight hours. That would break down to $375.00 per group or $31.25 per hour per person. Thus, you would be making $187.50 per hour. The teen group we run is not as profitable due to the insurance payment. The numbers for that break down in this manner. Group is 1.5 hours X the insurance payment of $22.50 (for the 1.5 hours) X the number of participants is (8) eight, equals $180.00 per group session. That comes out to $120.00/per hr. I hope that you are seeing how groups can add to your bottom line.

- Do not be apologetic about your fees or schedule. State your fees and leave it at that. You deserve to be paid for your time. If you need to do more work about money issues, do it. If the client can't fit into your schedule, it is okay to say, "Gosh, I wish I saw clients on Fridays too, but that time is reserved for my family, so, will next Wednesday at 5:00 still work?" We must remember to set and keep healthy boundaries as therapists and role model them for our clients. Practice this. You must get comfortable with it.

Another consideration when setting your fee is, *What can the local market bear?* Talk to other therapists, or scout out area practitioners' fees on the internet via their web pages and their listings on Psychology Today.com to get an idea of the average in your area. Your fees can be adjusted by trial and error, but don't start out undercutting yourself. Remember, you have a master's degree; you have thousands of hours of internship experience, all that you have learned since. That is a *lot* of personal investment in your chosen career; keep that in mind when determining your value. I mean, if someone is willing to pay a personal trainer $50.00 for a 30-minute torture session, will they be willing to pay their highly educated, highly trained, and experienced therapist at least as well? The answer is yes.

How many people live in your city? If you don't know, Google it. In my City of Riverside, CA for 2017, the population is 303,871. Of course, in more rural areas the population could be much less. However, you only need about twenty to thirty people per week to become paying clients to make your practice successful. Thinking of it in smaller terms can make it easier to ask for what you need. Additionally, you should know that according to Mental Health America in 2017, there are over 40 million people who have a mental health condition that translates into one in five people. Again, think about it, you only need a small number of those people coming into your office.

I know many graduate programs talk about giving back to society and providing for the greater good; and they stress providing free or low-cost therapy for those in need. I am all for that, but we, too, must make a living wage to be able to create the lifestyle that gives us the ability to give back. You and your business must be secure first.

Many therapists get squeamish when they are asked what they think their time is worth. If you are one of them, then it's

Chapter 6: The numbers

crucial to do some personal work around your personal money issues.

Here are some thoughts to ponder:

- What did your parents tell you about money?
- Did you have enough as a child, as an adult? Was there ever enough? What does "enough" mean to you?
- Do you doubt your value? If so, add more value to your service.
- You feel you must see seven clients in a day, but you are at your absolute best with five, then see five clients. You will feel better when you are doing your best work.
- Are you fearful you can't find clients who can/will pay at your rate? (Yes, of course, you are.)

It is important to work out your subconscious money issues now, or you will struggle with them repeatedly. So, here is an example of how you might ask for what you are worth.

Client: Do you offer counseling services for anxiety?

Therapist: Yes, we do. Can you provide me with a little bit more information? (This is used to determine if you feel the client will be a good fit for you.)

Therapist: (After you hear potential client and you want them as a client.) It sounds like I can help you. Can I tell you how I work? (wait)

Client: Um, sure, that would be great.

Therapist practice in a box

Therapist: My sessions are___ number of minutes. I find that for anxiety clients, working weekly really helps to decrease the symptoms of (list back the symptoms they gave you). My fee is $_____. I have appointments as early as_____. May I schedule an appointment for you? (Now wait to allow the client to think.)

The client is thinking and then may ask any of the following:

1. Do you take insurance?
2. Sure, let's set up the appointment
3. Ok, um, that is a little more than I can pay. (At this point, you can remind them it is an investment in themselves, or talk about their money objections. (Sometimes I remind them of their Health Savings Account or the ability to use their PPO insurance.)

4. If they still object to the cost, I refer them on and wish them well. I have had several clients call back after speaking with another therapist, saying "I felt you really got me" or that they felt I "was a better fit."

The important thing to remember is to be yourself. Say it with confidence even if you are not feeling that way inside. The more practice you have with this, the better and easier it will become. Practice stating your fee, again and again. Make it second nature. Find your words for this interaction.

Some coaches even have folks practice asking for more money than when you ask for less (your fee), it is an amount you are comfortable asking for. You will develop the ability to require your worth over time. Learning to charge what you're worth, or ask for what you need, is like exercising a muscle regularly to keep it strong.

Here are some books I've found helpful:

- *You're a Bad Ass* by Jen Sincero. Excellent book for self- doubt. She will have a new book; *You're a Bad Ass at Making Money*, which will be published in April 2017.
- *Get Rich, Lucky Bitch* by Denise Duffield-Thomas (one of the best books on money I have read)
- *Tapping into Wealth* by Margaret M. Lynch
- *To Sell is Human* by Daniel Pink.
  This book is great to help us develop a new mindset and get over the internal stigma we may have around selling. If you only chose one from this list, make it this one!

  It takes time to work through money issues, but once you are on the other side, it will be well worth it. Please take the time to ponder this; your overall success depends on it.

Return on Investment (ROI):

This is the amount gained for the cost. The math looks like this: ROI = the gain from the investment minus the cost of investment, divided by the cost of investment.

It would operationalize as the following:

ROI= <u>(Gain from Investment-Cost of investment)</u>
Cost of Investment

If you earn $30,250 (gross profits) from counseling services for the first quarter, (3 months).

Then you spend $1300 on Google Ads words during this quarter, plus operational overhead cost (rent, utilities, supplies, staff, etc.) of $3025 the total cost of investment would be = $4,325.

Say you obtain 4 clients a month from the ad, about 1 per week; with a net gain of 11 clients. This adds $30,250 gross profit to your business.

The math would look like this.

Example: $30,250 - $4,325.00 = $25,925 ÷ $4,325 = **599.42% (ROI)**

As you can see, this investment was highly profitable for my business. You must track your numbers.

Step 6: Start Getting Comfortable with Numbers

There are numbers in every business that you should know, and counseling or therapy business is no different. Below is a list of those you should start keeping track off.

Average number of sessions (ANS):

How many sessions does each client typically complete with you? Do you typically see a client, ten sessions, 20 sessions, or even longer? It will depend on the type of therapy you are doing and the concerns that brought the client into therapy in the first place. Nevertheless, you should have an idea of an average. I have a friend who does Employee Assistance Program (EAP) referrals, and his average is about four sessions per referred client. He recently figured that about 25% of his monthly clients stayed on as self-referred clients and the average is about 12 sessions. He does no marketing, but his calendar is full. He is happy with his 22 to 26 clients a week. He can then figure the value of each client. In my center, on average across all my staff, the average is around 25 sessions per client. There are a few outliers that I do not add in (remember statistic class?) These range from brief assessments that take only one or two sessions, to clients with a more serious mental health problem who may stay with you for years. Leave those out; they will mess up the average.

For now, start to keep track of the number of sessions a client attends to determine the average.

Average Client Lifetime Value (CLV):

Do you know the average amount each client brings in? If you know the average number of sessions per client, then it's about math. If a client attends 25 sessions at the $100.00/per session, the lifetime value of that client is $2,500, (gross). Knowing this number is helpful when you are planning your yearly projections, and it helps you decide if some of your marketing efforts are worth the cost. Knowing this number will help you understand how much it costs you to acquire a new client.

The Cost to Acquire a New Client (CAC):

In business, there is a saying that it costs more to obtain a new client than keep an existing client. The longer you have that particular client, the less, it cost you to acquire them. For example, we ran a Google AdWords campaign. It cost us $325.00 a month, and we brought in two or three clients per month. We ran the ad for four months. Therefore, the math looked like this: Total cost of the Ad: $1300.00. We received a total of 11 new clients, so the cost per client was $118.18. The lower the number to acquire a client, the higher the profits. This is not the end of the story you must also look at the Average Client Lifetime Value.

Working Capital:

This is the amount of money you have to work with on a daily basis. You can calculate this by subtracting current liabilities from current assets. This is cash-flow working capital. Strive to have $1.50 to $2.00 of assets for every $1.00 of debt. This number will change daily, but use it as a guide to help you plan whether to make a purchase or not.

Revenues:

Keep track of your sales (client services) on a monthly, quarterly, and year-to-date basis. Use these numbers to help set a goal, and monitor achievements. Know the difference between Total Gross (before expenses) and Net (after expenses).

Profit Margin:

This number will tell you if you are making money (profit) or losing money (loss). To calculate this, subtract all of your administrative and general costs from your gross profit; then divide that number by the number of clients/or products (sales). If the number is positive, hooray! If it's negative? Well, you have some work to do. There will be times that you will have a negative number. That is part of business. Do not give up. Create a workable plan to either bring in more revenue or reducedebt.

Chapter 6: The numbers

Know Your Sources of Referrals:

Where are your people coming from? Who are your top 5 referrals sources? Where is your web traffic coming from? Ask your clients, "How did you hear about us, a specific website or through a general web search?" Maybe it's a speaking engagement you did last week or networking with your peers for the specific event you attended? Measure and record. The good news is that my EMR keeps track of my referral sources and my Google Analytics keeps track of my website visitors. I just need to look at the numbers on a regular basis. I should be able to ask you who are your top five referral sources. This is another number you should know.

Keep track of the referral sources that fuel your business. Ask all your clients what site or person told them about you, it could be a referral from the doctor or the minister or maybe your well- written Psychology Today profile spoke to them, or they Googled "therapy" in your city and found your excellent website. Why do you want to keep track of these things?

1. To find out what is working and what is not working.

2. To be able to replicate what is working.

3. To nurture the referral sources.

4. To set a plan to fix what is not working so well.

5. To know if the marketing venue is worth the money

Profit and Loss Statement:

This is the document that you should be reviewing each month. You need to know what you spent and how much money came in. Knowing this number can help you track whether your ads are paying off, how much to set aside for expenses, how much you are making, and if you can pay yourself a wage. You, your bookkeeper, or accountant should print this out monthly.

Time to check In, Are You Ready to Quit Yet?

I sure hope not. Take a deep breath and know you can't do it all in a day, a week, a month or even in a year. It is okay to take this one step at a time. You will move forward, and your dream to open a successful private practice will come true. Just do one thing a day toward your goal. Maybe it's to read a page in this or another book. Maybe it's to call a few people and tell them about your practice. Maybe it's going to a network meeting or writing a blog. There is always something you can do. Can't-do one thing a day?

That is alright, how about one item off the list every two days or even once a week? What I am trying to convey to you is that sometimes progress is slow and other times it will be fast. There are weeks that you may be emotionally ready to work hard and other weeks where your tank is just empty. Please honor that process and give yourself some grace. What healers do on a daily basis is phenomenal, and sometimes our work can't be on any timetable. Also, once you have made the practice successful, you will want to tweak it every year. As humans, we never fully arrive for long. We are always in the process of planning, evaluating, modifying, and implementing. Do celebrate your successes along the way and celebrate both the small and large victories. Go back and review your wins. The process is hard along the way and looking to our successes helps with motivation.

Chapter 6: The numbers

Please take a little time to list three of your victories
here as of Date:_____

1._____

_____

_____

_____

2._____

_____

_____

_____

3._____

_____

_____

_____

Additional wins as of_____(date)

1._____

_____

_____

_____

2._____

_____

_____

_____

3._____

_____

_____

_____

Check List of To Do Items

☐ *Open a Checking and Savings Account; look for a free business account.*

☐ *Review tax status and find an accountant or bookkeeper.*

☐ *Find an accounting software and start using it. An accountant can help set it up for you.*

☐ *Stay focused on your to-do list; install a time management app if you need extra help.*

☐ *Set your fee; do research on your competition and determine how much you need to make.*

☐ *Figure out the number of clients you can/should see in a day, week, month.*

☐ *Sit with the numbers, develop a system to track the numbers, get comfortable with them.*

Courage is a love affair with the unknown.

—Osho

Chapter 7: Insurance

Step 1: Malpractice Insurance

Malpractice Insurance is an absolute must, and it's a legal requirement. Malpractice insurance is designed for healthcare employees or other professionals like attorneys and psychotherapists. It covers you in the event a claim is filed against you. Thank goodness, the claim rate for therapists is low, and thus the cost of insurance is not that high. For a few hundred dollars, you can purchase sufficient coverage. The amount you purchase should cover at least $1,000,000 for each claim and up to a $3,000,000 aggregate for total claims paid during the policy year. If you are doing a specific type of therapy, say sex offenders or sex therapy, you may want to consider higher amounts. We have a therapy dog in my office, and we pay a small addition for her coverage, too. Malpractice insurance will cover as needed your defense costs, deposition representation, as well as license protection. Please do not cut corners in this area; it's very important.

Shop around for coverage and be sure to check all professional organizations that you belong to. They often have policies available to members. The California Association of Marriage and Family Therapist (CAMFT) provides free malpractice insurance to students. Below are other choices that you have.

Chapter 7: Insurance

Resources: Malpractice

HPSO: www.hpso.com

CPH & Associates: www.cphins.com

NASW Assurance:
www.naswassurance.org/professionals/

General Liability Insurance

This type of insurance is often called slip and fall insurance; it covers your office space and the people who come in and out of your office. Say you have a water delivery man and he slips on the stairs delivering water. He could sue you, the building owner, and his company. Or one of your clients slips on a wet floor or sits in a chair that breaks, spilling hot coffee on themselves. There is a lot that can go wrong. In my experience, it is not likely, but it *can* happen. Remember the Scouts' motto! Always *Be Prepared*. You want your business to survive should you be sued for something small. Get this insurance. It's a must.

Step 2: It's A Choice Whether to Accept Client Insurance

We are now at a point to discuss client insurance. Some therapists love it because it brings in clients in return for a set rate. The rate, however, is often lower than you would normally charge. The trade-off is having a steady stream of referrals. That can be helpful, especially in the beginning as you are building your practice. Some therapists hate to market and network, so insurance is fine with them. I have a friend who works only part-time. She feels it's not important to market because she is happy with the number of clients she receives from the insurance companies. Still, there are other therapists who swear off insurance completely because it doesn't pay what they consider a fair rate. Some practice/business coaches recommend not taking insurance from the start and building only a cash practice. There are still others that do a combination of both cash and insurance. In 2010, with the advent of the new Patient Protection and Affordable Care Act (PPACA), commonly called the Affordable Care Act (ACA) or, colloquially called Obamacare, one of the main features is that this law has given most Americans access to health care who might not otherwise have it. An example, of qualified individuals who are included, are small business owners like us, but also some medium-size business and retirees who did not qualify for their state Medicare programs. ACA as it stands also allows for my two college-age children to retain their insurance through my plan until they are 26 years old. Additionally, this bill limits the overall health insurance costs that companies can charge for their plans. No matter what your political affiliation or feeling about this bill, it has made sweeping changes throughout healthcare. What that means for mental health professionals is that more people have access to healthcare and many people want to use their health insurance. Currently, in 2017, this entire process is up in the air. It looks like the ACA will stay for 2017, and after that, unfortunately, it's anybody's guess. But know there will be some changes. It may be a good time for new therapists to work more on obtaining cash pay clients at least until the dust settles. I do know many therapists who want to take insurance clients because they feel it is their calling and they, too, like to use their personal insurance when they are seeing healthcare providers. If that is you, wonderful, just stay on top of what the current administration is doing so, you will be prepared.

However, there are people who do not want to use their insurance because they are concerned about their jobs. I have many first responders, military, and government officials who do not want to use their insurance because they do not want any record of a mental health transaction. Another reason that people will pay cash is that they have a high deductible, and it's better to pay your rate. Still, other people will have heard of you and your skills and want to come see YOU, and they are willing to pay cash for the pleasure of working with you. If you have a good reputation in your specialty, clients will frequently elect to pay cash just to see you. This would be a great goal to set.

Find out what is best for you; there is no right or wrong answer. We each have to decide to take insurance or not. In my group practice, we decided to take a few insurances (4 companies); what I call "insurance light" as well as cash pay. We were selective in picking which insurance companies we were willing to work with. My partners and I wanted to provide care to people in our community who were experiencing some type of trauma. We applied for the R3Continuum formerly known as Crisis Care Network. My colleagues and I have always worked in the trauma field, and we understand what is needed in this area. This type of work is short-term and provides an immediate way of helping.

With this insurance panel, we also got on Employee Assistance Programs (EAP) where you see clients for three to six sessions to resolve one concern. Often these are work-related, such as a co-worker suicide, or management/employee fights. However, it could also be a divorce, drinking on the job, stress at home, work or school. The focus is usually crisis-oriented and short term. After treatment has concluded the employee may self-refer back to you if things come up later. Please read all insurance contracts carefully, as some will permit self-referrals and others will not. I have even had EAP folks give my name or my company to their family and friends. It's important to remember that any person you have contact with is a potential client or referral source for you. Always do your best work.

Verify Insurance Coverage

If you do take insurance, please verify coverage before treatment begins. Learn about deductibles, copays, coinsurance, parity, and whether someone needs a referral to see you. The fastest way not to get paid is to take on someone in crisis, not understand their insurance, and then discover that their insurance won't pay you. Insurance is different for each company that contracts with them. It can also differ if they are management or a general employee.

There are "carve-outs," for example, if a client has HealthNet insurance and you are a HealthNet provider, you call HealthNet to determine coverage, and HealthNet tells you that they "carve out" their mental health piece to MHN. Then you must start the process over, and now you must call MHN to see if the client is covered even though their insurance card clearly states they have HealthNet. You will need to ask about your client's co-pays, yearly deductibles if there is co-insurance and where to send a claim. If you are using an electronic clearinghouse, and I would suggest that you do, ask the insurance representative for their payer ID number for the clearinghouse you intend to use. Here are some other considerations for insurance on special circumstances.

- What do you do if the client has a victim of crime claim and they have insurance? Know that Victims of Crimes' cases in most states are the payer of last resort. Therefore, you must have a denial from the primary insurance company before the claim will be paid by Victims of Crime.

- How many sessions does an EAP referral have and when do I file my claims? Beware that most EAP companies give you three to five sessions. Plus, many EAP companies only allow a 60-day window to get your claim into them for payment.

Insurance can be a profitable way to partially fund your practice if you know the pitfalls and do your best to avoid them. When I was first starting out, I picked up the book *Navigating the Insurance Maze: The Therapist's Complete Guide to Working with Insurance -- And Whether You Should."* by Barbara Griswold, LMFT. I wore that book out learning about insurance and how to bill. You see, when I first started out, I called a few billers and was told that their charge was 8% to 11 %. One biller told me that for $10,000, she would get me credentialed and on as many insurance panels as I wanted. I was utterly astonished—my total budget was $10,000— and I couldn't possibly spend it on that. Maybe if I had spent that money my practice growth might have been faster, but who knows? Even today, when I can afford that, I still wouldn't spend that much, and I hope you won't either. What I would recommend if you want to take insurance is to please buy a copy of the *"Navigating the Insurance Maze: The Therapist's Complete*

Therapist practice in a box

Guide to Working with Insurance -- And Whether You Should."
by Barbara Griswold on her website:
http://theinsurancemaze.com/store/.

She also has other products you should check out: about ICD-10 codes, claim forms, billing service referrals, and more. She also does speaking engagements, and she is a cool person. What a win-win! I would suggest that if you are thinking about insurance to read her book cover to cover and you can even do this without having a practice. I read her book about three months before I started my practice. That way I was well on my way to the knowledge I needed before I took my first insurance payment.

A couple more things:

1. Please collect the co-pay, religiously. It is very important and will add significantly to your cash flow. Also, it will keep you out of a dual relationship: of being a therapist and banker to your clients, which is a huge ethical concern. Your clients should never owe you more than 2-3 sessions worth at a time. I also bill the intake the day I do it. That way I know quickly when there is a problem. And, I bill monthly for all subsequent sessions.

2. Take a copy of the front and back of the insurance card and the client's driver's license. Keep the copies in the clinical case file.

3. When you call the insurance company, ask for the name of the person you are speaking to, note the day and time of the conversation and keep that in the clinical file. Twice, I have had an insurance company go back and listen to the recording of a call to determine what their customer service person quoted

125

me for the benefit information they provided and both times I have "won" and received payments for services I later rendered based on information given to me.

If you have decided "No Way! I'm not taking insurance," fantastic; you get to move on to the next section. However, if you are not sure or are interested in the hybrid type of practice with limited insurance, then please read on.

Take these steps if you are applying to be on insurance panels.

Note: It will take each insurance company a few months to process the paperwork; on average, it takes about 90 days before they will place you on their referral panel. In fact, I have had at least two insurance companies take over a year to process my application. If you do not have a physical office space yet, use your home address or a box until you get credentialed. Once you have a physical space, you can change your address. Further, not this process often is two-fold, one is the application/Credentialing and the second part is contracting. Both need to be done and often are on separate time frames.

Step 2A: Apply for an NPI

A National Provider Identifier (NPI) is a unique 10-digit identification number given to all healthcare providers in the United States. It is part of the Health Insurance Portability and Accountability Act of 1996 (HIPAA) and the office of Centers for Medicare and Medicaid Services (CMS). This number specifically identifies you as a healthcare professional. This number is a number for life and no matter where you practice, this number will follow you. You may already have one if you ever worked for County Mental Health or other agencies. You will need this number even if you are not billing insurance directly. You can Google your name and NPI to see if you already have one. If you do not have an NPI; have no fear getting a number is easy. Go to

National Provider Identifier at
https://nppes.cms.hhs.gov/NPPES/Welcome.do

If you provide a superbill, this number is often required. It will take you about 20 minutes to complete the application and then you are emailed an NPI number. Note this number is for life and will transfer with you to any other practice or locations.

Step 2B: Apply for a CAQH profile

Next, you need to complete a profile on the Council for Affordable Quality Healthcare (CAQH) Data source. This non-profit organization obtains and holds all your credentialing information. It is used by some insurance companies to keep their credentials current on you. Every 120 days you must update your information and data in this system. If the insurance company uses this system, it will save you time and shorten their individual application process. When you fill the information out for the first time, you will need to check Aetna (they are a default insurance company, and you need at least one to complete the paperwork) as the insurance company for which you are applying. Aetna may or may not be an insurance company you want to participate with, but it will get you registered into this system.

Otherwise, you will have to wait until insurance companies ask for your ID. Registering for Aetna shortens the process. When you are first starting out anything you can do early is a good thing. Remember it will take about an hour to complete the application. Here is the link: http://www.caqh.org

Calling Insurance Companies

Once you have decided on which insurance companies you would like to apply to, call their Provider Relations desk and ask about their application process, and whether they are taking new providers in your area. Sometimes just by calling I was allowed on a few panels because of my specialties in trauma, PTSD and working with children, and because I was on the phone I was able to talk to a real person and persuade them to accept me. Other questions to ask when you have them on the phone are:

- What is their process; is there both a credentialing department and a contracts department?

- What documents will they need from you? One insurance company asked for a copy of my transcripts. Most, however, only need a degree date and major.

- How long will your application take to process? Often you will be referred to their website to complete the application. When we first started out, we applied for EAP companies, as it was easier to get on their panel and they had quicker approval time, less paperwork, and most paid fairly well. As time went on, we have reduced the number of insurance companies we take, but the first year it did help.

- Ask if this person will be your representative and how can you contact them if you have further questions.

- Ask about how to get your checks direct deposited with

electronic fund deposit. This will save time and get your money into your business quicker. Think cash flow.

Make sure you take a photocopy of everything you send to them. Keep all fax transmittals to prove you have sent the documents; this step alone has kept my application alive. I didn't have to redo everything. Follow up with them in about 30 days to see where your application is in the process.

Credentialing

Here is a list of what insurance companies, who don't use the CAQH system, may want from you.

- Copy of your driver's license

- Copy of your degree (graduate)

- A copy of the license to practice within your state

- Resume

- Advanced or specialized training

- W-9

- NPI number

- EIN number

- Application

- Malpractice Insurance

Step 3: Credit Cards, Part of the Cost of Doing Business

It is extremely important to set up a way for you to take credit cards. I know when I was first starting my business, I was looking around and I thought that wow, I have to pay 3.75%

plus 15 cents to run the card. How could I afford that? Are you kidding me? Here is the deal, you need to be able to give your client a quick, convenient way to pay you. Our society likes fast, fast, fast, so not having the ability to collect credit cards will hurt your business.

Plus, the more you charge with your merchant, the lower the fee becomes. In California and many other states, you <u>can't</u> pass the processing fee onto the customer. Just think of it as a business expense and move on. You do get to take it off your taxes. Stop worrying about that small fee. Do check around for the best possible rates. I would also suggest you calendar a yearly check to determine if you still have the best rate and to reevaluate your credit card merchant services; as your income increases the rates may go down. In my business, we use a service called Square to complete our credit cards and payroll services. You can find Square at the link <u>www.Squareup.com.</u>

When you use this link, you can **Process your first $1,000 without fees when you activate with my invite link: https://squareup.com/i/AE42B81F.**

(If you use that link, I too, will receive additional processing for free; so, thank you for all that are willing to try it.) The benefits we enjoy from Square are ease of service, low fees, quick payouts (cash flow), and the ability to be mobile. We also use Stripe for some of our website purchases because it integrates well with WordPress (the popular website builder) and it has an easy interface, low rates, and quick payout. If you are a member of Costco or another warehouse store or a member of a professional association, such a National Association of Social Workers (NASW), you can sometimes get good deals on rates. It does pay to check around. Pun intended.

Therapist practice in a box

The major, easy pay, credit card companies to check on are:

1. Square: We have used them for many years and find it to be easy and straightforward, even with the new EVM chips.

2. Stripe: We also use it for several of our websites that we have. Again, easy and not too costly, especially when you are starting out. This one directly integrates with our EMR.
3. PayPal: We use this service for a few products on our different sites.

There are other merchant services out there, but the ones I have listed are designed specifically to provide very good rates to small businesses, and they don't charge thousands of dollars. Remember at some point you will be making several thousand dollars through these accounts. Please evaluate all fees and costs, depending on your total sale costs and find the program that works for you. Credit cards and debit cards are an easy way to obtain your client's co-pays. Also make sure your merchant service takes Health Savings Accounts (HAS) or Flexible Spending Accounts (FSA) many companies offer these types of accounts to their employees, allowing the employee to use pre-tax dollars.

One more thing, if you decide to use an EMR most have the credit card company already integrated into their system. I would seriously look at that company. This will save you time because the payment information goes directly into the client's file. Thereby making tracking of payments quick and easy. Remember automation is the key to creating systems for your business.

Check List of To Do Items

☐ *Obtain malpractice insurance: YOU MUST HAVE THIS BEFORE YOU SEE ANY CLIENTS.*

☐ *Depending on where you rent your office space, you may need General Liability insurance (slip & fall) or renter's insurance. Call a few insurance brokers and talk to them about your needs— better safe than sorry.*

☐ *Will you take client insurance or not? Think long and hard about this. Talk to other clinicians in your area. Join Facebook groups; be selective in your list.*

☐ *Read,* Navigating the Insurance Maze *by Barbara Griswold.*

☐ *Apply for CAQH if you are going to accept insurance.*

☐ *Apply for an NPI number.*

☐ *Get all your credentialing documents together in a folder. If you are applying for insurances, this will make your life so much easier.*

☐ *Review referral sources. You should have at least 5. If not, network more. If you are taking insurance, locate an additional 10 referrals' sources as rates for insurance are lower.*

Therapist practice in a box

☐ If private pay works out, plan to do networking weekly. Set up a schedule of speaking, or pop-ups, go out into the community & talk to people about what you do. Example: Doctor's or Lawyer's offices, schools, PTA/PTO, YWCA. (Think: where do my ideal clients hang out and what other professionals do they work with.) That is where you start with popups.

☐ Review credit card rates and sign up.

"Marketing is really just about sharing your passion."

- Michael Hyatt

Chapter 8: Marketing

Marketing is a term used for any activity that helps manage the process by which goods and services move from the concept idea to the consumer and everything in between. This also includes determining price, promotion, and development of goods or services. Below are some steps that will help you stand out from the crowd.

Step1: Marketing Planning, Getting your Name out

It is a good idea to begin to settle into some type of marketing plan. By that I mean you must develop a structure to get your name out into the world. There are people out there who need you and the wonderful service you provide; they just need to find you. Thus, it is your job to let others know who you are, where you are, and what great services you provide. Think about how you might reach them. Think about what is uniquely you, and what can you bring to the community that no one else can. Now I know you might be thinking "I'm just a therapist, an intern, I have nothing that is unique." I assure you, we all have our own gifts and abilities. We just sometimes need to define them. We all have our own personal experiences. Graduate school prepared us to do the work, but who we are at our core, including all of our combined professional training, every client experience, good or bad, accumulates into the secret source of our gifts. This information is what we must convey to our prospective clients, that we alone own bring individualized characteristics to the table, each of us is uniquely different.

Chapter 8: Marketing

How do we share this with the world? Once we figure that out, we will have clients.

Free Online Directories

The first step is to list your business in as many online directories as you can. First, look at the free directories like Google My Business Account, formerly My Places (a must: to get your business on the map), Yelp, Bing, Yahoo Yellow Pages, Health Grades, Local city, Mantra, etc. Let's do a little exercise right now. Go to Google, type in "therapists" or "counselors" and your city (ex. therapists + Riverside). Google brings up a map and lists the top three; if you click on "more," you will find 20 or so more listings. However, in my area, the word "therapists" also brings up physical therapists' listings, as well. Try other combinations, like "counselor, marriage, and family counselor, couple's counseling," etc. So how do you get on this list? It's very simple: to go to www.google.com/business/ then click "start now" and carefully fill out all the information.

Make sure all the information listed in all the directories is the same. You don't want your address listed wrong or the hours listed incorrectly or even photos of two different office buildings. All listings should have the current, accurate information. Wrong or outdated information is very frustrating to our clients and may even decrease SEO rankings. Google will then have you verify your business and who you are before publishing the listing. I would not pay extra for the "executive member listings," as they often cost hundreds of dollars and you can pretty much do it yourself.

Again, remember to update your listings if you move or your website address or phone number changes. Also, add photos and as much information as you can to complete the listing. It is helpful for your SEO ranking and to have outside backlinks to your website. When you get to add the part about your business, speak directly to your ideal client. Explain how you can help them and that you understand their pain.

TIPS:

• Remember to calendar a time *yearly* to go back and look at all your directories to make sure all the information is current. Do it now…. please. Additionally, as you make updates to your website, the new information needs to be refreshed in Google. Google uses bots (AKA Spiders) that are crawling the internet looking for index information. The more Google understands what your website is about, and who it serves, the easier time clients will have in finding you and you will be ranked higher in the search. This translates into being listed the first page or two of Google; which is a highly desirable place to be. Please note, it may take Google three to four weeks to update your information and change your page ranking.

• Make a list of directories you have signed up for, including the usernames and passwords. That will make it easier to update and add items yearly.

Paid Listings

These can be worth it if you want to stand out in the crowd. The current ones to look at include:

Psychology Today (https://therapists.psychologytoday.com/)
Good Therapy (http://www.goodtherapy.org)
Theravive (http://www.theravive.com),

Chapter 8: Marketing

Network Therapy (http://www.networktherapy.com) Therapy Tribe (https://www.therapytribe.com).

These paid listings run about $300.00 to $400.00 per year and can provide referrals to your practice. People who use these sites can connect to you even when your business is closed. These services are most helpful to the client, and you, if you follow these tips.

1. Make sure to position your website and phone number in an easy-to-find place in the directory listing.

2. Put as many photos on the site as you can and add a video if possible. At the very least, make sure your photo is on the site. Not the small one with you standing on the top of the mountain; the one where they can see your eyes (think head and shoulders). Please remember that clients connect to people, not to pretty sunsets and trees. There are too many therapists who fail to put a photo on the site and hide behind all their education and accolades. A potential client wants to know you and how you will help them, not what college you attended. All that stuff makes it harder for clients to connect with you. Remember clients are looking to connect to see if you "really get them."

3. Write the copy for these sites directly to your ideal client. Write it to help solve the pain point of your client. In some areas, there are a lot of therapists, i.e., a lot of competition for clients. That's okay. The clients who need to find you will if you speak to their pain. Tell them how you can help them. You will stand out from the crowd by writing good copy to the ideal client and including photos to share your office with them. If you are still uncertain about putting yourself out there, don't be; you have worked long and hard to get

to this point. You have what it takes, and you *must* believe in yourself and your skills.

(You Got this!)

- List your title and your tagline (in short, what you do). Here are some examples: Jane Smith, LCSW, the Angry Teen Tamer and Parenting Partner; or David Alexander, LMFT, The Anxiety Banisher, Co-parenting Referee, and Tantrum Dissolver.

- Complete the entire profile and double check the information for accuracy. Some listings can add more zip codes searching. List all the local ones to help boost the search results.

- List only three or four specialties; you CAN'T be a specialist in everything! Would you go to a therapist who had 20 specialties? If you said yes, to that question, then think about this: If you had a heart problem would you go to a podiatrist or cardiologist, both are doctors? Clients are more sophisticated, and they want the specialist to treat them. be that for them.

TIPS:

- Many therapists complain about paid listings, but they are a great marketing tool if used correctly. Make sure you have a photo, a video if possible, and speak to your ideal client. Your degree or modality of therapy is not as important as who you are and what can you do to help your potential client. Think "How I can help a potential client get out of pain?"

- I recommend using at least one paid service, like Psychology Today, for a couple of reasons. PT and other paid listings are very large and have wonderful SEO (Search Engine

Optimization). If you are on their service and your website is listed, the PT site will link to your website. This provides a great connection to help with your listing. It gives Google another way to know what your website is about, which again will help with you getting found. The cost for PT service is a $30.00 per month commitment plus some foreign transaction fee (look for credit cards that do not charge a foreign fee). PT's company is in the Cayman Islands. Other paid services range from $25.00 a month up to $300.00 a year. Some offer CEUs for low cost or free, others have a magazine, or allow you to post videos and articles on your profile. Take a look at the other therapists, can you tell what they offer and who they are talking about? If you were a client would you call them? Write your profile to your client and then they will call you. Write the profile to everyone, and nobody calls you.

Step 2: Your Website

Every therapist needs a website. Yes, you do. You must have pictures of your office, of you and the staff, and you must tell folks what you do. The internet is a great place for potential clients to check you out and "try you on" before they call. You want your website to be on the first page or at least the first couple of pages on Google or Bing or other search engines. This is where SEO or Search Engine Optimization allows your website to be indexed or found. Having a high SEO ranking is a critical component to your success. I am not a computer wizard, and I do not know HTML (Hypertext Markup Language) A.K.A. computer speak. I can Google certain HTML codes for basic stuff and you can too. However, I have a great website and so should you. It is easy to spend $3,000 or more on your website, but when I was starting out, I couldn't afford that. So, I went the less expense drag-and-drop method and used a small company that offered basic templates. It worked because at least we had a website and many therapists didn't have one at the time. Now I will admit, it wasn't very pretty, and it was basic. We eventually outgrew that site and needed an upgrade.

Believe me, your website is always a work in progress, and it should be ever-changing. I have used designers for websites and web developers to help with Wordpress sites, which I find somewhat complicated. We currently use the Squarespace platform for one of our sites, which is another but much more advanced drag-and-drop platform that I find easy to use. We also have a couple Wordpress sites that I often use YouTube to help me manage. However, if you are not a techie there are services that will help you or will build it for you, such as Brighter Vision. Other site builders include some hosting companies, or there are courses you can take to design your own site. For example, check out Zynnyme.com. These wonderful ladies provide this course for free for therapists, and they put on great training. Bottom-line: you MUST have a website and a very good one.

What should you have on your website?

TOP 10 Items for your website

1. List all contact information, so it's easy to find. I recommend offering email, phone number, and texting info, if possible since many clients find it less stressful to text that first inquiry. Don't forget your address! The bottom of the web page (footer) is a great place to put this information. No potential client should have to hunt down how to call you or find your office location. Make it easy for them.

Chapter 8: Marketing

2. Address your ideal client in all your web copy. Remember the client's avatar that you developed in Chapter 2? When you are writing the copy, see them in your head. I sometimes visualize them across the table from me as I am writing. Be specific on how you can help. Let them know you understand their pain and you "get" them. A clear description of what you do, who you help, and why you are the one they should select for your service is a must. Many therapists start off with their credentials as being important. Not so. I get it, you worked very hard for your degree, and you survived the licensing process, or you're in the licensing process. Clients might care about your degree and if you're qualified, but they are more interested in if you can really help them. Help solve the client's pain. I know this process can be scary. Please trust me and the process. When you have that ideal client, all this work will be worth it.

3. Use clear descriptions for your navigational links on each web page. If the page is about anxiety, speak to that. When listing staff or contacts or adding your specialty or service pages, please be detailed in your descriptions and tags. Each page will have a meta tag. Meta tags are words of the text that describes the page's content. You will not see Meta tags they are in the code of the page. Also, make sure you add your keywords to each page. This helps Google and other search engines to find your pages.

4. Adding keywords in your copy on your website is a requirement as it will help people find you. For example, when a person is searching for "anxiety in Riverside, CA"

my counseling office pops up on the first page of the search results in Google. You want that outcome also. Think about the clients who will be searching to find you. What is your specialty? Where are you located? Did you know that the term therapy is searched four times more than counseling?

How do you find your keywords, you ask? Google Key Word planner is one such tool. You will first have to set up a Google AdWords account, and it is very helpful for this. It's free, and you may someday use their AdWords for marketing. But for now, let's just use the tool to find what words people are using to find "marital therapy." First, you target your geographic location. It won't help to search for marital therapy in other parts of the world if your client comes into your office for therapy. If you are selling products, online therapy, or video services, then you might want a broader base to review. Let me show you how this works I typed into the search bar "Marital Therapy" and my location, and the following information was listed:

Couples therapy: 49,500 searches
Couples Counseling: 49,500 searches
Marriage Counseling: 12,100 searches
Family therapy: 880 searches

These searches are per month in my geographical area. Notice "Marital Therapy" was not even listed in the top 4 or even the top 20 on the total list? Thus, if you wrote a blog or copy for your website and you offer counseling for couples you would be far better off by listing the service as couple's therapy, couple counseling, or marriage therapy instead of marital therapy. Use the keywords and sprinkle them throughout your copy in a natural and well-written way; not just thrown in the article to move up in SEO. It will help people find you, and you will rank higher in SEO. Add six to eight keywords in your copy. I do this by writing the copy first and then as I am editing it, I will go back and add more keywords if I didn't use enough initially. I will also use the keywords in the titles and headings of the page; again, do it in the most natural way possible.

Another very cool way to find what people are actually

typing into the search engine bar to find services is located at the bottom of the page under the title "Searches Related to_____ (fill in the search terms). In the picture above, I typed in "Couples + Riverside, CA" into the search engine bar. If you scroll all the way, you will find these other keywords searches that people were looking for. these might be good additional keywords that you might want to incorporate if they are relevant. Other FREE keywords tools: Google Trends or Keyword Tool. Both will help you decide what your keywords might want to incorporate if they are relevant. Other FREE keywords tools: Google Trends or Keyword Tool.

Both will help you decide what your keywords these might be good additional keywords that you might want to incorporate if they are relevant. Other FREE keywords tools: Google Trends or Keyword Tool. Both will help you decide what your keywords should be.

5. Avoid therapy reviews on websites as they are ethically difficult for a therapist to use properly. In California and many other states, you can't use testimonials, as ethics boards feel they will mislead clients. However, if you are selling products or a class, you can use testimonials (think psychoeducational, not therapy).

If you use an outcome measure scale, inform potential clients about your results. One such scale is Scott Miller's Outcome Measure. http://www.scottdmiller.com/performance-metrics/. You could say 80% of your clients' report feeling better after six sessions of therapy, based on the specific outcome measure you use. Please keep a copy of the aggregate data to be able to prove your claim if you use this. We do use outcome measures. We are careful about using this tactic; we only advertise the numbers that we have good data for. We do specifically spell out in our social media policy that we do not encourage our clients to leave feedback on Yelp or other social media sites. We encourage them to keep confidentiality in mind. However, our clients may want to spread the good news about you and your company. On this point, please check with your professional associations or licensing boards. No one wants to be in trouble over something so small.

6. An embedded Google map of your location on your website is a must. A Google map is easy to embed in your website and will make finding your place so much easier. It will also give Google an easier way to find you and provide you with higher rankings in SEO. Sign up for a business account, and you can get the code for your website. If you need more help with this here is the link to Google's map instructions. (http://bit.ly/2xqzZ6K)

7. Use photos and videos if possible of your office, inside and outside on your website, social media and profile directories. This will make it easier for potential clients to walk in the door that very first time. In the file names of the photos make sure you have your counseling name and location. This tagging is another way for the Google bots or spiders to classify your pages. These bots are sent from Google to your pages where the bots scan your pages and send information back to Google. Once Google understands what your pages are about it will link your information. Thus, boosting your overall SEO. An example

of this might be a photo of you with Susie Smith Counseling + Santa Rosa, CA. Also, add a description whenever possible. If you are using WordPress, you can add plugins such as SEO Pressor, SEO Cleaner or WordPress SEO by Yoast. If you have a Squarespace or Wix sites, you can type in the metadata and descriptions.

8. Create a video for your website. Speak directly to your client and how you can help them. Now I can hear you; you're saying: "What? A video? Are you freak'n kidding me?" Nope, I am not kidding you. Take out that fancy phone of yours and start talking. Again, it doesn't have to be a fancy phone or a video camera; you can use the web camera on your computer. Just speak to the client as if they are standing right in front of you. Visualize them, and you are just answering their questions, imagine it and speak to them. WAIT... STOP THAT HEAD TRASH.... I can hear it: "I'm fat, my hair is not right, I'm much better in person, I can't talk in front of the camera, I have no clothes to wear." ALL EXCUSES. Please hear me out. Your client is in pain; they are upset. If they are coming in for marriage therapy research says they have been thinking about therapy for close to six years before finally taking the first step. What a video does is allow them to hear your voice, and connect with you; it's like "trying you on" before they start the process. Hearing and seeing you may help them decided that you are you a good fit for them and that you will understand their problem. The client could care less if your hair is too long, too short, too gray, or you are too anything_____ (fill in the blank.) Here is the bottom line: a client wants a human to connect with, and you are that caring, empathic, well-

educated, space-holding human. Create a one to two-minute video; that is all. Be yourself, smile, and just talk to them. Then upload it to YouTube and link it back to your website and other social media. One of my therapist friends links her email signature to her video. She has had her video shared many times because she comes across as so genuine.

9. Link to Facebook, Snapchat, Instagram, Twitter, or whatever social media your ideal client is using. If you don't know, ask them. More on Social Media later (See page 131).

10. Develop a logo for your business. Do you have one? If not, get one. Go to 99 Designs; for around $300.00 they will mock up a few options for you. If you are really on a shoestring budget, try Fiverr.com. Just remember that this site can be a hit and miss, but many "gigs" AKA jobs start out at $5.00. You most likely will have to combine a few gigs to get your logo, but for about $50.00 you can get a cool design. It does pay to look around and have a little bit of an idea before you tell a designer to create you a logo. Add your logo to your website. (See page 73)

11. (Bonus) Pay for good hosting. I know you are on a shoestring budget, but please pay for good hosting for your website. When a person is in pain and searching for a therapist, they are in a hurry. If your web page loads slowly they will leave and may not come back. Try to go for the gold standard of a 2-second load or at the very most 3-4 seconds for loading time. Make sure photos are compressed, all the links work, and each page loads properly.

12. (Bonus Plus) Add Google Analytics.
    (http://Google.com/Analytics) to your website. This
    great FREE program will provide you with a wealth of
    information as you build your business. It tracks the
    traffic to your website. It will tell you how many unique
    visitors your site has, what search engines they are
    coming from, how long they stayed on what pages, what
    days and times they visited, and much more. Try to get
    into the habit of reviewing these data monthly.

Do not let this long list overwhelm you! (A moment of
motivation: "You got this, really, you do. Keep taking steps even
if they are just one small step at a time.")

Building a website does not have to be that hard. Remember it
will never be 100% perfect. Just get something up on your
website, there is never anything that is perfect. Stop
procrastinating to make everything perfect. Know that you will
go back later and upgrade it. I have one cautionary note: if
possible do not use cookie cutter sites. These sites all look the
same and have the same number and type of pages. These sites
are lackluster and do not have a personal feel to them.
However, if you are not tech savvy or you already have a site
like this, don't fret; they are better than no website and clients
will still find you, which is the purpose of the website. Just do a
new website, once you have more money and time. If you have
this type of site, at least update it with your personal written
copy. Also, remember websites will change over time and
evolve, think of your website as a living and breathing thing
that needs care and attention at times.

Lastly, please have friends, family, and colleagues you trust to
look over your website and provide feedback about the ease of
navigation, photos, copy (including spelling) and have them try

using the contact links to see if the forms/files work. Do all the links work? Do this at least every six months to evaluate the site. You should also be adding content weekly or at least every couple of weeks to keep your website fresh. If you get into that habit early on, it will pay off with great SEO. Put "add and update my website" on your calendar now!

TIPS:

- Make sure the photos are legally yours, or you have purchased them from a stock photo company.
- Free photos sites: Pixabay, Unsplash, and Flickr offer photos through Creative Commons. Works by allowing you to use the photo if you provide attribution; listing the site as the source.
- Remember – in order to rank higher with SEO, link the photos to your site. For example, location+counseling+niche+file. Depending on what I am linking it to on my site, it could read *Riversidecounselingcoparentingclass (link in the tags).*

Step 3: Social Media

Social media are platforms that you can use to get your business message out there. Unless you have been living under a rock, you have at least heard of social media, and I would guess many of you reading this already use social media for at least staying connected to your family and friends. I am now asking you to consider using some form of social media to tell other people about your business and engage your audience, so they get to know, like and trust you and see just how great you are.

Therapist practice in a box

Note: It is crucial to have a social media policy for your practice. This policy should be in writing, and it should be client-focused and spell out your use of social media. For example, in my paperwork, I explain that I will not "friend" clients or like their pages on Facebook. I will not engage with them in a discussion if it leads to others knowing that they are a client. I further explain that I will never ask them to "like" our page or to list any reviews on any business-related page in which I promote my therapy practice. (This does not include the separate part of my business of coaching therapists, which does not fall under the same confidentiality rules.)

If a client chooses to "like" us on our therapy practice page that is their decision, but they need to understand that they are potentially giving up their right to privacy. It seems that the younger generation (aka under 35) are fine with liking our business page or engaging with us through our blogs or posting reviews. Younger people seem to have less concern about privacy and feel good about sharing their experiences working with us. I have had many clients say "privacy is an illusion anyway. Besides, I want my friends to know you guys are the real deal." While I must say, I am flattered; I do believe that counselors must take a stand and let our clients know that their privacy is paramount to us. As you can see, it is a good idea with the ever-changing technology to keep your policy page updated.

You must think of social media as a long-term strategy for marketing your business. Social media can help with the following:

- Announce a new product, a new therapist on your team, a new group, blog post, or to build up buzz about you and your services.

151

- Demonstrate your expertise in your specialty.
- Allow customers to know about you without a large investment of time or money.
- Put you in front of a massive audience.

Who is online? According to Adweek, January 12, 2015. 179.7 million people use social media; with the largest group of 35.3 million between the ages of 18-34. The second largest group is 29.7 million users who are in the 35-44 age range. If you are not media savvy, plan to learn to use at least two new media platforms over the next six months. Okay, but what platforms do you learn? Again, it depends on the demographics of your ideal client. Here is a summary of some of the current platforms at the time of this writing. New ones develop all the time, so keep up with the times.

Facebook:

Facebook had 160.9 million U.S. active users in 2016, with 1.79 billion users worldwide (source: Facebook 2016). It is one of the most dominant social media sites and allows you to create a detailed business page to attract clients to your practice. You can join for free and even run focused ads to target audiences and "boost" posts to get seen by more people. Facebook audiences range in age from 13 to 85. Here are some more fun facts from the Pew Research Center, for the week of March 17-April 12, 2015, about Facebook. (72% of all internet users were on Facebook)

- 77% Female
- 66% Male
- 82% ages 18-29
- 79% ages 30-49

- 64% ages 50-64

- 48% age 65+

- Engagement is higher on Thursday and Fridays

- 50% of the 18-24 years old go on Facebook as soon as they wake up

Facebook users are highly engaged, and over 70% of users are on the platform daily, compared to 59% on Instagram, 38% on Twitter, 27% on Pinterest, and 22% in LinkedIn. Facebook users are online an estimated time of 39 minutes each time they log in.

Pinterest:

Pinterest is a great platform to use if you have good images and content. Think scrapbook. This could work for those of you who are thinking about designing How-To checklists or creating How-to-step-by-step guides. Pair with an engaging photo and these pins can attract attention. You can also create "Rich Pins." These are pins that include extra information on the Pin itself. There are six different types of Rich Pins, but the ones most helpful for counselors are articles and product pins. Once someone pins the image, the web address associated with that pin can serve to draw in new clients. Pinterest users are:

- Mostly female (80%), although male usage is up within the last year or two.
- Close to two million registered users, with over one million active users, spending an average of 14.5 seconds each visit.
- Over 45 million users in the United States.
- Close to 68% Millennials (born roughly in years

1980- 2000).

- 20% have incomes over $75,000.

- Pins shared by moms are 3x more likely than other users to be shared.

- The Z generation (those born from 1990-2010) overall, use 27% monthly.

- 75% of users are on mobile devices. (Another reason you need a mobile presence, and your website must be mobile-enabled too).

- Creators of Rich Pins such as a recipe, or articles for counselors, get a lot more views and likes.

- If you list a product—another form of a Rich Pin—you will drive 36% more traffic to you.

- 93% of Pinners purchased a product online within the last six months.

If you are considering using Pinterest as a platform, please review this excellent article by a therapist friend of mine, Sharon Martin, LCSW: "*How I used Pinterest to Drive Thousands of Visitors to My Therapy Website*" September 26, 2016. Here is the link: http://bit.ly/2ecIqHl

Twitter:

There were 57.3 million users in the U.S. in 2016 despite the fact that posts are limited to 140 characters. It's a great platform to share opinions and develop personal branding. Users by age are: 18-28, 37%; 30-49, 25%; 50-64. 12%; 65+, 10%. Engagement rates for business to consumer is highest on weekends and Wednesdays.

Instagram:

Instagram (owned by Facebook) is an image-driven social sharing site that supports images, videos, and has a business page feature that lets you create a business page. This platform uses hashtags (#) to make it searchable. It had 65.3 million U.S. users in 2016, with a worldwide reach of 300 million Daily Active Users (DAU). It grew out of an app just for IOS users (Apple). Now it's a major social media platform for all devices, including Android. 51% percent of users are male, and 49% are female; with 90% of Instagram users' younger than 35. Instagram helps you get your message out quickly and offers a visual of your office, helping attract potential clients. You can show the fun side of your company or the human side of who you are. It's great for showing staff and the interesting work that happens in your office. You can feature your employees working or providing a talk to a small group of people. Businesses often create photo contests. You will have to get creative in using Instagram since we can't show our clients: however, you could use it to "enlist support for mental health," "what depression looks like," or share about your specialty. The goal is to get those prospective clients engaged. You can list speaking engagements or products you offer. You can take a photo of where you are at a conference and have people check in. It goes without saying that confidentiality is always paramount. Thus, therapists must learn to use these platforms more creatively than other businesses.

Snapchat:

In 2015, Snapchat was ranked third most popular app behind Facebook and Instagram for Millennials (ages 18-34). People think this app is "cool." They use this app at least five times a day.

Snapchat is used to send photos, videos, and stories—400 million snaps a day! Think quick (10 seconds) visual communication. As of April 2016, there were 100 million active users, with Ireland having the highest adult usage. This would be good if you were going to market your online therapy practice to people living in Ireland. Thirty percent of users reported they use it because their parents don't. Thirty-five percent use Snapchat because the content disappears within 24 hours. If you use this platform, you must create a strong video narrative. You can provide live access to events you are hosting or promoting, offer special content to a private member in your audience, give your audience a private tour of your office, or create a special class or support group.

YouTube:

YouTube uses videos to engage their audience and is currently the largest media sharing site. YouTube states they have over a billion users that watch hundreds of millions of hours of video every day. The average time a consumer spends on YouTube per session is 40 minutes. The breakdown by age is:

81.9% of teens (14-17) of US internet users.
81% Millennials (18-35)
58% Gen X users (34-54)
43% Baby Boomers.

The largest group (18-49-year-old), use YouTube on their mobile devices. The greatest advantage I can see of this platform is for therapists to create videos that people shopping for a therapist can use to check you out, before making an investment. As a business, you can make vlogs about what you do or specific ways that solve problems. This powerful social media platform should be in your marketing arsenal. It is not expensive, and it is easy to use— all you need is a camera, like the one on your phone! There is also an in-platform editing tool that you can use to make your video look great in no time.

What kind of video do you create? You talk from the heart. How can you, the therapist, help your ideal client? What can you do to stop their pain and anguish? Tell them in a two to three-minute video about what you do. Show them your office. Tell them about a new exciting product or service you are offering. You are building your reputation and expertise. Another feature of YouTube allows you to store the video ("hosting" the video), then, link it to your website, thereby not decreasing your bandwidth on your website or making it crash or slow down your client's viewing speeds. The bottom line, videos work great and having them stored on YouTube reduces your need for storage and bandwidth. Remember the 10 questions you are writing about? (Page 37) The most asked questions about your area of specialty? I see a great video on those ten questions posted to your website. (What do most of your clients ask you?) You might break it down into two videos for easy viewing. Another video idea is to create a short video about the ways to help the client receive help before they even come to your office. Let's say you have a top three list of anxiety smashing tricks, 3 ways to bust through depression, or two ideas that help you speak better with your spouse. Think value. According to Social Media Today, videos have a higher click-through rate than texts, images, or banner ads. This becomes a no-brainer. Please add videos to your site.

LinkedIn:

LinkedIn is a professional connection platform that is used for direct networking with other professionals. Before you connect with people on LinkedIn, read the profile of the person you have a profile photo? Why would it make sense for you to reach out professionally to that particular person? Have they not posted in a long time? If that is the case, there may be a better way to contact them, or maybe you do not need to contact them at all.

However, depending on the degree of contact (how close to them your relationship is) people often do respond. I would stay within one to three degrees for contacts. Many people list a preferred way to be contacted; use that method. It can be through the LinkedIn message feature or email. Be aware that some people are not accepting any more contacts. Read the profile before sending out your request.

Google+:

Although Google+ is a recent player in the social media arena, it has over a million users and allows you to have a business page. I would not recommend you spend a great deal of time on this site unless your ideal client does. However, at the very least you should create your business page. It works by making circles of a friend, and you can post articles and links to your page.

This is a sample of what's out there, but as you can see, there are many useful types of social media at your disposal. I am not suggesting that you use *all* social media; that is just too much to tackle. But there are advantages to using some social media. Here is a list of the top six reasons to use social media:

1. Increased visibility, which translates into presenting yourself as an expert on a subject.

2. The ability for prospective clients to try you on before they reach out and invest in you, which gives you more opportunity to convert them to customers. It gives you

a human element.

3. Not too expensive to use as one marketing tool.

4. You can use your audience to improve your services, allowing quick feedback and the ability to respond quickly to complaints.

5. You can target your audience and drive traffic to your website or the product page.

6. Social Media boosts your SEO; the more active you are, the more likely clients can find you.

TIP:

You may use programs like Cavna https://www.canva.com, Wordswag (iPhone), Instameme (Android) to create memes. I use Cavna, the free version, a great deal. More importantly, play around with them until you find one you like, and then use it regularly to create content for your audience: aka clients. Think about important topics that they ask you questions about.

What's a meme?

A meme is a picture or graphic with words that are funny, relevant to the culture of the day, social and can be philosophical in content. With your business, think branding, include website, hashtags (#), colors used, business cards and logo. I have used memes to create a campaign, posting memes frequently. In 2016 I used the #2016dosomethinggood. Here is an example that I have created for my business. I also use meta tags and my counseling website in the photos. If these are going on social media, save the file name using your location and counseling name. It will help the internet find you easier.

If you like to see the *Best Memes of 2017, (so Far)*. Please go to https://www.thrillist.com/entertainment/nation/best-memes.2017.

Step 4: Blogs

A *consistent* blog presence is essential in developing your own voice and your expertise in your niche area. You can even start a blog in graduate school or when you are an intern. You can write 500-1500 words and, if you research information, which from time to time you should, cite your sources and write from the perspective of what you already know and what you may already share with clients. Think of what you often tell your clients or what they often ask you during your sessions. Blogs help with SEO, so your website is not static and provides you with a higher ranking. Blogs allow the client to hear your voice and thoughts even before they see you. It allows the client to determine whether the prospective client and you will be a good fit. Blogs that get read include titles that create lists, for example, *Top 3 Things to Lower Anxiety Today* or *Save Your Marriage in 5 Easy Steps.* Look at current trends and write from your perspective about how this trend affects your client. Think about when you are standing in line at the grocery store; you glance over to read the magazine. Which titles compel you to check out or maybe even purchase the magazine? Write about hot topics. People will read it because it's trending. If you can't think of anything to write just Google blog titles or topics and many articles will pop up. Pick one, and just start writing. Write on a subject that you know about or use one from a paper you wrote for graduate school. Bottom line just start and start today.

Other Writing Opportunities

HARO (Help A Reporter Out) *www.helpareporterout.com*

This service connects reporters from all over the English-speaking world to relevant subject matter experts. There are a few rules for this to work in your favor. You must be on their email list to respond. You also must be the one that looks through the list.

When you find one, you can respond with your article addressing the problem. Other tips are:

1. Respond quickly.

2. Make it easy for the reporter: provide site sources if any and your contact information. Write your response in the return email.

3. Do not send back an email saying, "I have this much experience," and "I can talk about this or that, just let me know what you want," Or "let's speak about that." You must remember they are on a short deadline and they will not have time to contact you to discuss what you "might: be able to bring to the article." Just make your response in the return email with your contact information, just in case, the reporter has more questions.

4. The response should address the topic, be complete and be relevant.

5. Don't pitch your other products or service.

6. Know you may not know if you are being quoted until after the fact. Make sure you have your Google Alerts on for your name. That will help with notifying you.

Why is this helpful for your practice? It gives you credibility and identifies you as an expert. Clients want to go to the expert in the area of their problem. It will help you get higher SEO, and when a potential client Googles your name, it will show up and help the client to get a better feel for who you are.

MuckRack *www.muckrack.com*

This service is similar to HARO in that it's looking for subject experts and helps to connect to media outlets and journalists. I have not personally used this service yet, but I have therapist friends who found it to be helpful to their practice.

Step 5: Network

The Elevator Speech

Tell everyone you are starting a practice. Tell your friends, relatives, your doctor, religious leader, child's teacher, the cashier at your grocery store—absolutely everyone with ears. Get your "elevator speech" down. Think of being in an elevator and the person next to you asks, "What do you do?" Can you in 30 seconds describe 1? Who you help/treat? 2. What problems do you solve? I know this might sound super easy, but it can take some time to get it to sound perfect. Write it down and practice saying it. You must be proficient and sound confident when you say it. You will be saying this over and over during your network marketing. The more you practice, the better it will sound. You can add more information as time permits. For my practice, my elevator speech is "I supervise and manage a small group practice. Being a group practice allows us to have many different specialties and we treat many problems. We do not treat eating disorders, chronic mental illnesses, such as schizophrenia, or court-ordered sexual perpetrators." I then often will ask, "Can you tell me how I might help you today?"

Look for Local Groups

Join groups to market to, such as the Chamber of Commerce, Business Networking International (BNI), Rotary Club, Kiwanis, Zonta (a worldwide organization of executives in business and the professions working together to advance the status of women), AAUW (American Association of University Women), an advocacy group, or wherever your ideal client might hang out.

We volunteer six times a year to speak at our local Rape Crisis Group. We get referrals from them for sexual assault victims (trauma is one of our specialties). We also see their staff for secondary trauma and self-care.

I have a secret to share, and I must come clean right now. I *hated* networking and making small talk and trying to "sell me." Really, I did. With practice, however, I actually began to enjoy it, just a little bit. At first, I would make deals with myself and say. "Tonight, I will talk to five new people"or "Eight new people this week." The more I did that, the better I got and the easier it became. I started to think more about how I can help others learn more about me. Suddenly, the concept of selling became easier and less intimidating. I'm not selling them a used car; I'm providing information about my services and in general about therapy. That seemed less hard. I also read the book by Daniel Pink "To Sell is Human." Mr. Pink related that when he talked to others, it was about our ability to persuade others. Is that not what we often do in the counseling room? We persuade others to try on new behaviors, to think about problems in a different manner, or meditate or be mindful. This book makes these concepts easy to understand.

Step6: Add A Video to Your Website

Making a video is easy and inexpensive to do yourself, but here again, we need to get out of our comfort zone. Video viewing is up and our brains like videos a lot. According to comScore, a media company that tracks online engagement, 45% of internet users have watched at least one video a month, and the average person is exposed to an average of 32 videos per month. Close to 100 million Internet users watch at least one video per day. And 90% of retail shoppers stated that a video played an <u>important role</u>

in their purchasing decision. Video watching is also up with executives, 75% of them told Forbes that at least once a week they watch work-related videos on business websites.[1] Mavsocial.com reported that in a survey conducted by the group Demand Metric 400, marketing and business professions were asked about video marketing. 52% preferred videos for building brand awareness and 45% for lead generation and 42% for online engagement.

Is video watching the same among all ages? It turns out that Millennials are the largest consumers of videos, accounting for more than 18% of the 204.2 million digital video views in the United States.[2] However, according to YouTube, it's not just the Millennial's viewing that has increased. YouTube added another category called "The Old's." It had a large upswing of video watching too. "The Old's" was not clearly defined by YouTube, but it looks like it includes anyone over the age of 40. Who knew?

These days you don't even need to have a video camera to take high-quality videos. Most phones have great cameras. I would suggest you practice a bit as you learn how to use the video features and please use a tripod to steady your camera. You do not want to make anyone seasick by bouncing around. There is even a teleprompter on Amazon that you can buy that is not very expensive. I tend to go low tech and write out what I want

---

[1] http://mavsocial.com/video-marketing-tips-stratgey/

[2] http://www.emarketer.com/Article/What-Millennials-Up-with-Digital- Video/1012939

to say and tape it to the wall behind the tripod. But often, I just speak directly from the heart without cue cards. Please note, at first this will feel awkward, and you may even feel embarrassed, but believe me, it gets easier with practice. Think about creating a few videos. Make an introductory video of who you are, why you do what you do, and how you help. Add tips and maybe even create a video blog (Vlog), a blog done via video. If you want to take a look at a good one, my friend and colleague Robyn D'Angelo, LMFT, The Happy Couple Expert, has capitalized on this concept. Check out her link: http://www.thehappycoupleexpert.com/blog

Are you ready to harness the power of video? Here are a few helpful hints:

- Create good content (think "What problem can I solve for my audience/clients?".)
- You don't have to be perfect in the video; we are all human.
- Create videos that are no longer than two to three minutes.
- Make sure your video can be seen on mobile devices as clients will watch longer on mobile.
- Create catchy titles (You have about 55 characters for a title on YouTube).
- Add Video to your title; it helps with search status.
- How-to videos are very popular.
- Always add a description of your video on YouTube as this adds with SEO and it lets the viewer know what they are going to see. If you really want to get good at indexing your video, take a look at another colleague of mine's video, Dustin NcCorchuk's ,9 steps to get high ranking on YouTube (http://bit.ly/2ybCuZL).

Record a test video and, play around with it. Look up videos that are like the one you have in mind and watch it; take notes! However, if your heart is still in your throat, I have your back. Another fabulous colleague of mind and the guy who shot my first video, Ernesto Segismundo, Jr., can help you. His company is called Fylmit.com. He is also a Licensed Marriage and Family Therapist, and he can help you set up your first video, and he easily calms you down. His videos are professionally shot, and more videos can be viewed at Fylmit.com YouTube. I recommend that you watch a few of these for inspiration and ideas. (Also, if you talk to Ernesto ask him about how his company got its name.)

To review, a video does not have to be a large financial investment; it can be a DIY project. You can also add an animation of your logo (Think Fiver), and if you use a video software program, like Camtasia by TechSmith or Power Director, to edit your videos, they will look amazing. You could even hire a Fiver person to edit your videos. Besides, I know you are creating videos in Snapchat, so use the power of video for your practice.

Step 7: Speaking Engagements

Think about where you can start spreading your magic. Who needs to hear your message and your words of encouragement? This could be done by giving a talk to your local place of worship, the PTA, the preschool, women's club, Rotary club, Kiwanis Club, gardening club, or Rape Crisis Center. There are literally hundreds of topics that you can speak on that a client could benefit from seeing and hearing you and your unique voice and perspective on a topic. Ask your friends, family, anyone who will talk to you about possible places to speak. Listen to your ideal client. Where do they hang out?

What clubs or organizations do they belong to or support? I am not suggesting you stalk them, but do find places they enjoy that would put you in front of other potential ideal clients. Do you have a signature talk about a topic, such as anxiety, depression, teen suicide, marriage strengthening, etc.? Whatever your specialty niche is, you have to develop a speech and get out there to find the people who <u>need</u> you and what you have to offer. You may have to speak at two to three different places in order to get a return on your investment.

This brings up a good reminder: track where your clients are coming from (know referral sources). Ask them how they heard about you. That information is invaluable to know where to put your money and energy

Step 8: Google Analytics

This is an important marketing and evaluation tool to have at your disposal. Google Analytics measures how well your website and social media are performing; it provides information, including:

- How many unique visitors came to your site?
- How long were they on each page?
- What search engines did the visitors come from?
- What keywords are attracting them to your site?
- Engagement (length of time on a page or action taken).
- Location of your visitors.

Google Analytics is easy to install on your website and will provide you with great information. However, if you are not a techie or the sound of installing anything like HTML makes your eyes roll back into your head, don't do this task yourself. Have it done by someone. I get it, you are now thinking,

"Where will I find yet another person and how much will this cost?" Relax, go to **Fiverr,** https://www.fiverr.com/FIVER. You will be able to find a person to do this if your web designer didn't already install it.

Just Get Started.....please

- Keep a schedule to post on your two social media sites, calendar your social media time to make sure it happens. If you are new to all social media, set aside 15 minutes a week to create content and post.
- Bookmark all your social media sites to make them easier to find. A password manager is helpful.
- Use a social media manager; many are free. Look at Hootsuite, Buffer (the one I use), Meet Edger, SocialOomph, Spout Social or there are a host of others. These just make posting content easier as you load up the content and the program automatically posts it on your schedule.
- Use at least one social media site but aim for two. Select the one that your ideal clients use.

Fiverr:

This website is worth its weight in gold, offering many services from folks all over the planet. For about $5.00 a "Gig" (aka a job) you will find people who can do almost anything. I have used Fiver to create animations of my logos for videos, ($35.00 for three different ones with music!), create a PayPal button ($15.00), and email transfers ($5.00) among other things. When you type in your Gig, review the work of the person listing their ability. On the site, you will find reviews and the number of people who used that service. Get a feel for the person and where they are located. I use a guy in Bangladesh, and he is awesome, but the time zone difference is a factor. I would send him a message and then overnight he would respond. The quality of services for me has been great. However, a couple of my therapist friends' have had a couple of concerns over work they commission. But hey, for the money, it is worth a try. There are also other services like the former O-Desk which is now UpWork and Guru.com, among others.

Step 9: Develop Marketing Goals for Your Business

As you develop your marketing plan and execute that plan, you need to set goals. Is it unrealistic to expect 20 new clients from a speaking engagement (see page 146) or a blog article? (See page 140) If you speak to a very large crowd and 1000 people there were your ideal clients, then, 20 may not be unrealistic. However, if you have a 20-person audience, you get a call from three. I would call that success. The point is, setting a goal is a must. Take time to write down a few goals. I write my goals daily. Did you know that goals are more likely to happen if you write them down? A study completed by Gail Matthews at Dominican University showed that people who wrote down their goals accomplished significantly more than those who did not.

In a class I teach for new, county social workers I explain how to write SMART goals.

Therapist practice in a box

S: Specific (What area am I targeting?) Describe a specific behavioral outcome that will result in achievement of the goal.

M: Measurable (Quantity or a measure of progress.) This must include some easily discernible criteria from which achievement can be measured.

A: Achievable (How can it be done given the resources at hand). The goal can stretch you, but it must be able to be done. This allows you to look for possibilities that may have previously been overlooked.

R: Relevant (or result focused.) Pick a goal that matters to your business and that fits into your goals. It must be important to you.

T: Time sensitive or time-bound (How long will it take to reach the goal?) How much time is reasonable to accomplish the goal?

I would suggest you practice writing down a few goals and plugging them into the SMART system. For example:

Goal #1: I want to have three new, full-paying clients by the end of the month or by the end of the quarter, April 30, 2016, (Specific).

I will know if my goal is completed when I have three new, full- paying clients by month's end, (measurable). I will achieve this goal by attending 3 networking events and speaking to 5 new people about my services (Achievable).

Is obtaining three clients realistic? This seems like a realistic goal. Maybe not 25 new clients but three sounds doable.

Three new clients are important to your business success as they will bring in $3000* (Relevant). (*Average amount of a client's worth).

By the end of the month (30 days) I will have 3 new clients that have to attend intakes and set follow-up appointments. This gives you a reasonable amount to accomplish that goal.

What are the detailed steps you will take to achieve that goal? Here are a few ideas.

The plan to achieve the goal:

- I will blog weekly and post on my social media sites.
- I will update my Psychology Today Profile, speaking to my ideal client, by a certain date:____
- I will return all my phone calls promptly; within six hours, 10 hours, or 24 hours.
- Attend 3 networking events monthly and speak to five new people.
- Speak at a community event.

Step 10: Evaluation

How to Evaluate If the Marketing Plan is Working:

At the end of the month reevaluate the goal. Was it too easy? Was it too hard? Did you achieve the goal? Did you celebrate your success? This piece is very important as it helps create momentum and motivation. It's a secret ingredient, so to speak, of building a successful private practice. I have a whiteboard in my office and am always writing down the next goal I want to achieve. Whether it's the amount of money I want to make, the number of pages I need to write, the tasks I want to get done, or the steps I am taking to complete a project, I write it down! Plus, we know from research we are more likely to achieve our goals just by writing them down.

So maybe you are not the write-it-down type of person; that's okay, no judgment here. There are other ways to evaluate your success. One simple way to judge if you are growing are these questions: Am I better off this week than last week, last month, last quarter? *Am I better off this year than last?* The answers will depend on what you are measuring. First, we are a business, so we must measure our income. Did you make more? Track it. You can't make changes if you don't know what point we are starting from. I know the first couple of months we were in business it seemed like no money came in, but money was always going out.

At times, it still feels that way, especially when we take the leap to grow. It can be scary. One of our major growth times was when we met our goal of expanding our office space. The suite right next door to our current office came available at just the right moment, and by removing a door, adding a window, and removing a wall, we connected to three new offices. Before we made the deal, however, we calculated the added expense by the square foot. We thought about it a lot, envisioned what it could look like and how many more clients we would need to make it profitable. We were excited and scared all at the same time, but we did our calculations and took an informed leap. It was a measured and calculated risk.

You will have many of these types of decisions during your business growth period. I often look at my numbers to see where the business stands and make changes and course corrections as needed. You must ask yourself every week: *"How is my business doing?"* *"What can I do to make it better?"* *"What do I need to change, if anything?"* Changes and corrections do not have to be huge. Sometimes it's the little things that make a big difference.

For example, maybe it's attending one networking meeting this month, and next month maybe you aim for two. Or it could be speaking at one event, then increasing it to two next month. There are lots of moving parts to business; Be open to changes and sometimes doing things differently. Learn to be a bit uncomfortable, be courageous.

Therapist practice in a box

Check List of to do items

☐ *Begin to formulate a marketing plan: include referrals, network opportunities, directories, personal statements, use office and personal photos.*

☐ *Get your practice listed on all the directories you possibly can.*

☐ *Use paid listings: include your personal statement, speak directly to your ideal client, and include photos and videos if possible.*

☐ *Website: look at which platform to use, determine whether you are going to do it yourself or hire a web designer. A well-laid out website will pay back its cost many times over. Make sure you have a great website!*

☐ *Start by designing a website, write copy, and speak to your ideal client's pain point. Look for photos that have people in them. Potential clients connect with people. This is not to say you can't put in nature photos on your website, but people connect to people.*

☐ *Start a Social Media plan. Choose two platforms and learn them inside and out. Post regularly and often.*

Use a manager to schedule posts. (Remember automation.)

☐ *Blogs. Remember the top 10 list of Q & A within your niche? (See page 36) Answer 3 of those questions in your first blog. Post it to your website and social media.*

☐ *Blogs help with SEO. Post consistently every week, every two weeks, or monthly; post, post and post some more!*

☐ *Experiment with videos. Make one you're happy with and upload it to your site and anywhere else you can. Put in your budget to have a professional video shot once you start making a nice profit; in year 2 or 3. Until then, shoot videos yourself; it will help you tell your story.*

☐ *Develop goals around your marketing. You need at least five referrals sources; 10 if you are taking insurance.*

☐ *Add Google Analytics to your website and review the numbers monthly. Who is referring to you? How many unique visitors do you have?*

Everything in life is constantly moving and changing. Life is about embracing this change. For change is the only sure thing in life. —Mimi Ikonm

Chapter 9: Fine-Tune Your Practice

Once you are up and running, you will want to fine-tune the process. Sit in the waiting room and be a client. How is the experience? How is the vibe in the office? Can you make it more comfortable and welcoming, perhaps with water, flowers, and/or snacks? Is the seating adequate, comfortable, lighting good? Is the payment process easy? Is filling out forms online or on paper convenient? Does the client feel valued?

Go through your office procedures with a critical eye. Can your lower overhead costs by automating certain tasks? Would a Virtual Assistant help? Thereby allowing you to see more clients and thus bring in income. Think through the process and see if you can reduce barriers and streamline your processes to become a well-oiled machine. Not in terms of personality, but in the process of systems. Can you lower the overhead by automation?

Look at reducing the cost to increase your bottom line. Can you use coupons to purchase office items you use every day? Look for even small ways to save; they will add up over time. Don't forget to think about growth. How can you add more clients, products or other services? Further, remember to calendar a yearly review of process, forms, insurance, planning and update the automation process, too. You can't fix everything all at once. I have a monthly goal to complete one review task per month.

Step 1: Hire a Coach

Another way to fine-tune your business might be to hire a business coach. Merriam-Webster defines a coach as "(a) private tutor, (b)one who instructs or trains, especially: one who instructs in the fundamentals and strategy." A good business coach can help you cut through some red tape and avoid some pitfalls, helping you to reach your goals more quickly than if you go it alone. I have used several coaches and found their help of great value. They have actually saved me money and, more importantly, they saved me time with the learning curve. While most coaches are not cheap, it's a worthwhile investment if they help you stay accountable and push you when you need it. Sometimes we just don't know what we don't know. A coach can give your practice, a second look and propel you further, faster.

Some coaches, like myself, work with people just starting out; others work with more advanced cases. There are business coaches who specialize in book or product launches, some in money blocks, and still others in upping the take home for an established business. I encourage you to consider a coach, even for a short time, to guide you past hurdles; or consider year-long mastermind groups. These can propel your business forward more quickly than you can imagine. However, do your homework and get references before spending money on a coach. Make sure you have an interview with them before you set up a contract. You and the coach must have a rapport. I had a friend who hired a coach and every time she got off the phone with her it took weeks for her to recover fully. This coach was abusive, under the guise of being "no-nonsense." She would yell at my friend, put her down, and even call her names under the pretense of motivation. That is not a productive relationship! I have been careful about who I work with and have had the opposite experience; my coaches have been supportive, kind, and care about what I am doing. They may have been no-nonsense and helped keep me accountable, but they understood me, and when I couldn't complete a task, we talked about the resistance and created a new plan. In your journey, there may be tears and new realizations that you have some personal work to do. After all, we are all humans and as such are always growing and developing. Do that personal work if that comes up for you. Creating a business can be hard, but highly rewarding work.

A coach's job is to work with you to create the extraordinary practice you want. As I said, you need to do your homework when choosing one. Look at the coach's website. Based on that, does this person resonate with you? Trust your gut. If the fee is too high, or the feeling just isn't right, walk away. There are a lot of coaches out there! Take the time to find the one who fits with you. You will not regret it!

Here are a few additional questions I ask a coach before I hire:

- How will we work together?
- What support do you have in place for me?
- Do you understand my vision? Are you running a business like the one I want?
- How much is this going to cost me?
- How long will this process take?
- What is the Return on Investment (ROI) that you

have seen for your clients?

- What can I expect? Ask questions if you don't understand.

If you want to work with me, please go to my website: http://therapistbox.com/products/

Step 2: Find Your Tribe

Another essential for creating a thriving private practice is your "tribe." Seth Godin defines a tribe from his bestselling book of the same name as: "a group of people connected to one another, connected to a leader and connected to an idea."

These tribe members may be from graduate school, your workplace, other therapists, neighbors, small business, etc. Tribe members have each other's backs, and they will give you the truth when you ask questions and seek advice. A tribe member is not your competition, but rather supporters of your work and business efforts. Please do not get into that negative headspace where you are looking at others with jealousy or envy. *You are the only person you should ever compare yourself to, and when you do, you should only, ask "Am I better today than yesterday?"* Your tribe will help keep you accountable. They will gently push you and tell you when you are whiney. They will also tell you when you have done great work. You do not need a huge tribe; 5 or 10 people will do. Start building those connections.

Step 3: Self-Care

I know you have been busy with the many steps of creating your ideal practice, but now I want you to take a moment to evaluate your self-care routine. As you may know, mental health professionals can experience burnout at the same rates as first responders. In one study done in 2009 by Bressi et al. the burnout rate is as high as 50% for mental health workers. A composite review of 15 studies (Lim et al., 2010) on burnout looked at over 3,600 mental health workers. It revealed that age was the most significant factor in experiencing emotional exhaustion. The highest category of burnout occurred by mental health professionals between the ages of 25-35. Interestingly, the lowest burn out rate was for those clinicians age 55 and higher. I guess there is something to be said for gaining wisdom with age. Additionally, this study found that the higher education a clinician had, the more likely they were to experience burnout. Burnout is serious. It can negatively affect our work with our clients, lead to chronic physical or emotional health conditions, addictive behaviors, and poor social interactions. Healers often have a hard time saying no and keeping boundaries. I urge you to keep self-care at the top of your to-do list. We all went to school for a long time, and we have put forth plenty of money, time, and hard work to get where we are. I would hate to see you throw it all away in only a few short years.

Here are a few gentle reminders for clinicians:

- Self-compassion
- Work with clients that you have a passion for
- Regular exercise
- Healthy diet
- Family and friend time
- Vacations
- Seeking consultation and peer support
- Join a professional organization
- Personal time for fun and relaxation

Chapter 9: Fine tune your practice

Finding balance is hard to do; but it is a part of our job, and while you are on this practice building journey, I want you to be mindful of your life balance. I often tell my clients that life balance is a lot like sitting on an exercise ball. You can be centered, but as you lean too far in one direction without recentering your position, you become unbalanced. This is normal and happens to all of us. Please do not dismiss this important concept. I know you teach this or something similar to your clients. I just feel it bears repeating as we get rolling along here.

TIP:

A great new thing I just discovered is the use of essential oils for self-care, and for clients, too. First used over 6,000 years by the ancient Chinese, Egyptians, Romans, and Greeks for cosmetics, perfumes, and drugs; these oils have been gaining in popularity over the past few years. Recent research seems to substantiate many of the claims about certain oils used in aromatherapy. These oils work by eliciting a mental, emotional, or physiologic response. The University of Minnesota, in their newsletter *Taking Charge of your Emotional Health*, (accessed 2017) described it this way:

> *"Interaction with the Limbic System (Emotional Brain) during inhalation, odor molecules travel through the nose and affect the brain through a variety of receptor sites, one of which is the limbic system, which is commonly referred to as the "emotional brain."*

Because oils are absorbed quickly through the skin, they can make a person feel different fast. The olfactory system is one of our senses that can trigger memories. Oils can quickly help lift a person's mood. In my practice, we use essential oils in our waiting rooms and in each treatment room if the client and therapist agree. In our waiting room, we use a eucalyptus and mint oil, or rosemary. Our clients often tell us they come early just to sit in our waiting room to relax. They love the smell, and it provides a sense of well-being.

Additionally, in a 2013 study conducted at the University of Northumbria in the UK essential oil could have an effect on boosting brain power. In this study, the researchers scented the room with Rosemary. They found the subjects performed better on word puzzles and memory tests than did the control group.

We have never had a client have allergy concerns with us using oils in such small amounts. If you use too much, the scent becomes overpowering. Plus, the cost can be prohibitive, so remember a little goes a long way. I have used lavender in my office to help a client with sleep issues and citrus to help elevate mood. These are not a replacement for medication or cognitive therapies. The National Institute of Health[3] said, "aromatherapy is used by patients primarily as supportive care for general well- being." Thus, essential oils do not cure but enhance care. Here is a list of some basic oils and their mood-enhancing properties:

- Bergamot can create a feeling of joy, freshness, and energy by improving the circulation of your blood, thereby enhancing overall mood. (Depression)

---

[3] https://www.ncbi.nlm.nih.gov/pubmed/22789792

- Lavender helps with anxiety, lowers stress, and improves overall mood. It is also known to help with sleep. A 2013 study of Lavender as a supportive therapy for the treatment of Post-Partum Depression, Generalized Anxiety and PTSD demonstrated a reduction of symptoms and found no adverse effects[4].

- Roman Chamomile can be used to promote calm and reduce stress.

- Frankincense is not just for Baby Jesus; it is also used for calming the mind, lifting the spirit, and enhancing the effects of meditation.

- Ylang Yang is an oddly-named oil said to provide relief for anger, stress, anxiety, and to strengthen the nervous system.

- Clary Sage can be used as a sedative and to reduce insomnia.

- Citrus properties include being uplifting, invigorating, and having anti-depressant qualities.

Again, I am not saying that essential oils should replace traditional therapy or medication. However, I do believe there is enough evidence for them to be used as an adjunct to therapy, so include them in your toolbox. Plus, they make your office smell really nice!

Step 4: Follow-Up with Referrals

At the end of each year, we send holiday cards to both our clients and the past year's referrals. The client cards are a simple "hope you are enjoying your holidays." Since it is not ethical to thank our referrals directly for a specific client, we just thank them for their referrals over the past year. That way we make sure we stay on their mind for the upcoming year. We include a few business cards, and we also send updates of new services and introductions of new therapists and their specialties. If our referral numbers start to dip, we will send an update of our practice to our referral base. In this postcard, we remind them of our services or share a new service or group that we are currently offering. We will send about 30 postcards out, and we have always gotten at least 5-8 referred clients back. If we figure the cost of the card, printing, address labels, stamps and a couple of hours of our time the total figure is about $100.00. If we receive, say five clients, and we know our average client stays with us 25 sessions and if we make $100.00 a session each client is worth around $2,500. This activity as you can see has high returns for us. We have noticed that people like to get postcards or other mail, it has become such a rarity with electronic everything. This has helped a great deal with client flow.

Step 5: Ask Your Clients What They Want

About every six months, I send a survey to all our current clients asking them how are things going. I use Survey Monkey, and I create my survey to be no more than eight questions. I get about a 45% return rate, with about 95% of the return being 100% satisfied. My questions include:

- Do you think your therapist understands you?

- Do you feel comfortable with your therapist?
- Does your therapist listen to you?
- Do you feel safe in our office?
- Is there anything we can do to make your experience better?
- Would you or have you recommended us to family or friends?
- Do you enjoy your group?
- Are there other services you would like us to provide?

The questionnaire can be answered 100% anonymously, but if they want feedback they can provide an email address, and I will follow up. In the years, I have done this survey I have gotten good information about services offered. We started doing a co-parenting class after a few clients asked for it via the survey. We also get snack suggestions when our waiting room snacks get boring. Surveying your clients can be a good way to add more value to your practice.

Step 6: Taking to Clients & Leaving the Door Open for Returning Clients

I talk to my clients about how they think our sessions are going about every 6 to 8 sessions. I want to make sure we are hitting their goals and working on what they came in for. We use a formal satisfactions tool that was designed and researched by Scott D. Miller's evidence-based scales, for monitoring the quality and outcome of health care. These scales are easy to use, and they help a client see how they are feeling at the start of therapy, middle of therapy and the end of therapy. Our clients

like seeing their progress and they can review it. Additionally, when we terminate a client we always leave the door open should they have additional issues to resolve or work on in the future. We have received clients back four, five, even eight years later. They came in saying it's now time again for therapy and they thank us for keeping the door open. We have given them permission to come back should the need arise.

Check List of To Do Items

☐Review your systems and streamline.

☐ Calendar recurrent tasks yearly: website updates, forms, office policies, insurance coverages.

☐ Hire a business coach to move more quickly your practice to a higher level.

☐ Find your tribe, the people you can bounce your ideas off of. They are there, find them.

☐ Add value to the office.

☐ Essential oils?

☐ Self-care continuously: Add vacation and time off to your calendar.

☐ Referrals follow-up.

☐ Ask clients what they want and create a survey.

☐ Evaluate the counseling process.

I always like to look on the optimistic side of life, but I am realistic enough to know that life is a complex matter. Walt Disney

Chapter 10: What if You're Still in Graduate School?

Are you still in graduate school? Studying, loving the theories, reading, participating in the class discussions, finding stimulation by just going to school? Are you soaking in all the techniques you possibly can? Graduate school is a wonderful time to learn and study and prepare yourself for this work.

Your dreams of helping people by using all your new skills make you happy and are highly satisfying. After all, you will be reducing pain and suffering in your community. You will be helping people who are "stuck" in their life, people that have no place to turn; you will be there for them. You will create a place of safety and security where they will find acceptance and relief. You dream of one day having a private practice.

Someday you will figure it all out and learn to become successful. All your classes are preparing you well. Plus, you're thoroughly enjoying the class that prepares you for business and practice building. You especially like that one. Wait... What? Didn't you have that practice building or business building class? Really, how can you be expected to create a marvelous business to help others without that? Oh no, what should you do? Don't fret. I didn't have that class either, and I have a thriving group practice. I want to share with you what I consider the top 10 things you can do today as a graduate student to start to build your practice.

1. **Write, write, and write some more.** I know you must write

papers on many different topics for classes. Save each one of them. This content often can be re-purposed to use in a blog or your website (which you will have), as memes for social media (See page139), or material to draw from when asked to be a guest blogger on someone's website. Maybe even write a blog for the professional organization that you belong to. This content can also be a springboard for you to start creating your own authority in a particular subject matter. I know you are thinking wait...what? I am only a student, an intern! What do I know about (fill in the blank)? You may now feel like you do not have the knowledge yet to be putting yourself out there. However, you do know more than the clients who would be coming to see you. You do have classroom time on the subject, research, discussion, and further research to write that paper or project, that, oh yeah, you received an "A" on.

Dustin Wax of Life Hack defines an expert in his article "How to Be an Expert (and Find One if You're Not)" http://bit.ly/2gduomV. He lists these attributes to becoming an expert: knowledge, experience, communication ability, connectedness, and curiosity. Those are all skills every graduate student I know has. I know you may be a little shy and uncertain about all those hours of experience you have gained, but bottom line: you are in graduate school. That makes you one of only 10.9 percent of the U.S. population with a graduate degree[4]. Therefore, you are one of an elite group qualifying for the expert status. Writing content for your blog or website will be different than a group project or term paper for school.

---

[4] 2012, U.S. Census Bureau Data

However, that content can be repurposed and modified to define your voice in the world. So, write and write some more; writing in graduate school keeps your writing skills in tip-top shape. I hear seasoned therapists say they should write more all the time! Keep up your writing momentum, and it will be easier to continue this wonderful skill.

2. **Start reading books on marketing and business.** Most likely you will not have any business classes in your graduate program. I am not suggesting you go back to school to earn your MBA, but you will need to self-educate in this area. I know you're already groaning; I can hear you saying "But Sherry, I am already reading a ton of material! I can't possibly read anymore!" I get it, I really do. I worked full-time and went to graduate school at night, taking two or three classes a term. It was, I do remember very hard, but I knew it was for the "short term." I will counter that with - you still have at least 20 minutes every couple of days, right? Did you notice I didn't say daily? You do not have to race through and devour a book a week. What I am saying is the "slow and steady wins the race" attitude will help you on this one. I find my time by using my daily commute to listen to audiobooks in my car. I listen to two or three books a month during my 15 to 25-minute commute! Its time reclaimed to build my business. I hear you saying: "But Sherry Audible costs $14.95 a month, right? I can't afford that. I am just a poor graduate student." Okay, here is another suggestion; if the fee is *prohibitive,* then in your community, there is a free public library that offers some digital services. They may not have all the latest books, but they will have some of the best business books. Plus, great business books never go out of style. Otherwise, most towns have at least one used bookstore, with plenty of

great books and CD books just waiting for you to read or listen to. Find a few minutes in your week for some pleasure business reading. Daily reading for 20 to 30 minutes is also a form of self-care. You need time to recharge your batteries away from your school work. Reading is a huge pleasure, and there are some fabulously well-written books in this area. Please, just find the time. Even if you only read on your school breaks, you can squeeze in a few business books a year. Below are a few more of my all-time favorites, to add to those already listed elsewhere in this book:

- *The E-Myth Revisited* by Michael Gerber
- *The 7 Habits of Highly Effective People: Powerful Lessons in Personal Change* by Stephen Covey
- *The Four-hour Work Week* by Tim Ferris
- *Tribes* by Seth Godin
- *The Virgin Way* by Richard Branson.

3. **Podcasts.** Most of these are free, and there are some very good ones on running a business. These are shorter than books, but they are often packed with wonderful tips and information. All you need to do is download a podcast player. You can find a podcast player at either the Google Play store or the Apple App store, and there are many different ones to choose. There are even stand-alone players you can download directly from the web. Here are some of my favorite podcasts, in no particular order:

- *Fire Nation* by John Lee Dumas (general

business)
- *Practice of the Practice* by Joe Sanok (Therapy practice building)
- *The Therapist Experience* (Therapy practice building)
- Gary Vee (Vaynerchuk's *The # Ask Gary Eve Show)*. (Business)
- Amy Porterfield's *Online Marketing Made Easy*. (Online marketing)
- Blissful Practice by Dr. Agnes Wainman (Therapy Practice Information)

4. **Network everywhere.** Always be on the lookout for opportunities to network with other professionals, and join professional groups. You'll find some on LinkedIn, Facebook, and listservs. You will get referrals from these contacts once these people get to know, like, and trust you. As a student, other professionals will form an opinion about you based on your interactions. These same people may be able to offer you a practicum or internship when the time comes. They may be able to provide you with a recommendation or at least a handshake that could open the door to a wonderful opportunity. When I was starting out, I received an introduction from a therapist to an attorney in my area. This relationship has developed over the years, and now this attorney serves on the non-profit board that I helped create. She is a fantastic asset as well as a good friend. Talk to everyone you can about you and your business. I tend to be a slight introvert, and at times this becomes a bit uncomfortable for me to do. I suspect the same thing will happen for you. I made a deal with myself to push myself in ways to get better at meeting with others. I set an intention

to talk with three people an event, get their business card, and follow -up with an email thanking them for our conversation. I wrote on their business card something that stood out about them. For example, "therapist, pink sweater, likes kids and elders." I tried to include something about the event and then a link to an article that they might like. Think added value. I still do that most of the time. Now I can afford to limit my networking to only a few events a month, but the premise is the same.

5. **Social Media.** Social media groups (See page 36) can be used in two-ways. First, find professional groups on Facebook that share practice tips, both for licensed and pre-licensed people. Try to contribute regularly and be polite and supportive when you are interacting with other members of the group. You will learn a great deal from these groups, and again, people will get to know you, and it will build your reputation. Second, look for groups of people you may want to work with. Look at the most common problems and the responses they receive from others. Say you are interested in grief and loss. Join a grief and loss therapy group and observe what the participants are saying. Learn to identify the problem and what they need to solve the problems. You will be way ahead when you start to put your website together, write a book, or set-up a speaking engagement. Another platform to consider is LinkedIn but use this mostly for professional contacts. This social media site is where your voice can be heard by posting your blogs for other people to read. This platform is also good for networking with colleagues. Try to contribute some content every few weeks. Be kind, polite, and NEVER be mean to anyone in any of these groups, it

just not good form to "diss" others in a public forum. It is fine to disagree and state your opinion, but always do it in a respectful, kind manner. A negative social image is a terrible thing to have.

6. **Free Training.** As a student, sometimes you have the opportunity to hear speakers or you can even volunteer for a conference in exchange for a free or reduced conference rate. Some of you may have joined professional organizations, such as CAMFT (California Association of Marriage and Family Therapist), ACA (American Counseling Association), or NASW (National Association of Social Workers). Many offer free or reduced-cost training opportunities as part of their membership. Keep a list of all the training you have taken. I keep all my training on an Excel spreadsheet. The columns I use include the date, the name of training, speaker, and a number of hours the training was. Then you can print it out and attach it to your resume when you are looking for that internship or employment position. It is a great document to have, plus if you get into this habit when you are licensed, you will have a system in place for tracking all your CEU hours. Just a side note: One big reason therapists get into trouble by licensing boards is failing to have the proper number of CEUs by the date they certify their renewal form. They sign up for some CEUs in the future, send off their renewal form, and then something happens, and they don't take the training. They now are short of the required number of CEUs by the date they signed their renewal form, thereby perjuring themselves. Don't do that. That is a fast way to become unlicensed or sanctioned.

7. **Photos.** It's always useful to have a ready supply of photos to be used for blogs, web postings, social media and articles that you write. This is the perfect time to start creating your collection. Cell phone cameras have improved to the point that they have replaced many SLR cameras. And really, who doesn't have their cell phone with them all the time? So, think about your blogs and what type of imagines you need. I enjoy traveling and often take photos of interesting scenes to use as backgrounds. Be sure to include colors, textures, and scenic pictures. Whether you're at the beach, in the mountains, at a street fair, or taking a walk in a park, take pictures! Then transfer them to your computer, and you have your personalized collection of free images. There are low-cost places to obtain high-quality photos if taking pictures is just not your thing, or if you need people or other images that you haven't taken yet. Creative Commons is a useful website for no or low-cost photos. Just remember to cite the photographer whose images you use. Other favorite free sites of mine include Pixabay, freedigitalphotos.net, and Unsplash. Depositphotos charges a small fee, but their images are well worth it. A word of caution about photos. You can't just copy and use any old image from Google, as many of them are copyrighted. I have a friend who used an image she found on the Internet for a flyer for a nonprofit event, and she received a $1500.00 bill for the use of one photo! Please use only photos you have legal access to. Here's how to find images that you can legally use. First, do a Google search, say, "Photos of bears." When the array of photos of bears pops up, look in the menu bar just above the pictures. On the far right, you will see a link called "Search tools." Click on that, and you will see a new menu below

it. Click on "Usage rights" for a pull-down menu that allows you to filter out photos that are not free to use. Those left are free. The photo you wanted may disappear, but infringing copyright is both rude and illegal! And while you're in that menu, here's another useful tip on image size. When you click on that pull-down menu, it will offer different sizes. The larger the size (number of pixels) the more clearly the image will reproduce. This is especially important for PowerPoint slides. If the image is too small, the perfect picture that looks so good while you're composing the slide on your computer screen will be fuzzy and useless when projected on the screen. Always use "large" size images for presentations. Another great place to look for photos is AppSumo. They offer discounts regularly on many apps, but photos apps are also included.

8. **Use all opportunities with clients.** Start defining who your ideal clients are (see page 39). I know that as a practicum student or an intern you may not be able to choose the type of client or issues that are assigned to you. Part of that is to provide the learning experience that all therapists should have, and partly because the site where you are working is most likely an agency or government clinic and they see all clients who are eligible. Regardless of your site, always make notes about how you feel internally when you are working with any client. Our training asks us to routinely check in with ourselves to determine what transference issues we may have with a client. We must be aware of the feelings that come up when the client tells us something, all while maintaining a professional demeanor.

Ask yourself these questions:

1. What kind of client leaves me filled with energy?

2. What kind of client leaves me feeling totally drained when they leave?

3. Who are the clients that make me sleepy or seem to suck the air out of the room?

4. What type of client problem resonates with me; what is interesting to me?

What I am asking you to do each and every time you see a client is to conduct market research. Every client is a potential source of information. When you study certain client concerns, what do you find most fascinating? What problems simply do not interest you or you have no desire to learn about? For me, I have learned that I enjoy working with couples and people who have experienced trauma or have anxiety. I do not work with clients who have eating disorders, as I feel out of my scope of practice with that population. These clients need a therapist with specialized training that I do not have nor am I interested in obtaining. I understand that you can't do this until you have at least some experience and spend some time with different clients, but use this time to think about what kind of client suits you best. Bottom-line: watch and learn.

9. **Create a top 10 list of your clients' most asked questions**. What are your clients asking you the most? Maybe they want to know how to reduce the panic attacks or why they are sweating so much. The information that a client gives you can compel you to write a blog, create a meme about reducing panic, or even write part of your website copy for that potential client. Thus, answering their questions even before they pick up the phone to call you.

Therapist practice in a box

Do remember not to use your client's name or any identifying information. Use a composite to create the top ten question's list. The list could include topics like: How long will counseling last? When will the depression lift? How does counseling work? It could be about specific ailments, such as "Is it normal to feel so depressed after a breakup?" "Will I ever feel normal again after my divorce?" Build this list over time. This information is invaluable and will help you with educational information that clients want to know. This is all good stuff.

And ...

Drum roll, please....

10. **Your spouse and kids are always priority number one;**

   ALWAYS. I know you are super busy; I was too—attending graduate school, studying, working, commuting, attending church, singing in a choir, raising twins, and participating in a long-term marriage. That list doesn't even have extended family or friends on it. I tried to keep in touch with my friends and see them when I could, but they had to wait sometimes. I know it's always hard trying to find the time, but remember graduate school will end, I promise. Next up will be the licensure hours you need to do. Focus on your family when you are with them. Forego other tasks to put them first. Keep your spouse informed about your schedule and what priorities you have. Find at least a little "couple time" each day. Years ago, my spouse and I started having our morning coffee together before the kids got up. No phone, no TV, just us talking about whatever came up. And we still do! Find time; you will be glad you did.

On their deathbeds, people don't think about
their work or their life experiences or the items
remaining on their to-do list. They think about
Love and Family- Rick Rubin

What to look for in an internship

When you're looking for an internship, make sure the site is going to give you the experience you want. Look at the agency's website. Know what they do and what counseling services they provide.

What will your duties be and who will you be working with (as in the type of clients)? Ask the interviewer lots of questions. You have a right to look the supervisor up on the BBS website or other state licensing boards. If you live in another state, please check your specific licensing board for what the supervisors' requirements are, then make sure the proposed supervisor has the hours and CEUs needed to be a supervisor. I always have a copy of my CEU certificate ready to show to prospective interns. However, never once has anyone asked to see it. I think that it is a good policy to ask, after all. I look up each intern and therapist with the BBS before I hire them to make certain they are in good standing. Why would you, the intern, not do the same? I have heard of terrible supervisors not providing signatures or not being available for supervision hours. Sometimes the agency has promised supervision only to find out that it's only after you pass a year's probation and are recommended by your supervisor. Talk about a bait and switch! An internship should be a fantastic learning experience. Ask about how the agencies' market themselves, and what you can do to help market the practice. Does their website have blogs you can add to? How do they handle social media? I would have at least 5 to 10 questions ready if the interviewer doesn't raise the issues in their discussion with you. Some that I would include:

- Is this a paid internship? If so, what is the rate of pay?
- Who will be my supervisor? If it's not the person interviewing me, when can I meet him/her?
- What will my hours and days be, and at what location (if they have more than one)?
- Will I be in the office by myself at any time?
- Who should I call in an emergency?
- What type of client problems can I expect?
- How many clients will be on my caseload?
- Do you use an EMR or what form of notes do I write, DAP, SOAP, Narrative notes? Find out, and do the research if you not familiar with that style.
- Will I be expected to find my own clients?
- Where do you find your clients?
- Will supervision be individual or a group?

Each site will be different, and not all these questions will have answers. For example, if you are applying to a county agency, they most likely will not need you to market or even write blogs for their website. Some counties in California don't even have an active website. A county agency is a great place to get hours and a ton of clinical experience, but won't give you much in the way of business skills. Find what works best for you. Remember these business skills can be learned. To have a stable stream of clients and excellent clinical supervision may be reason enough to take a government job. A good supervisor is crucial to help you develop into an awesome counselor.

TIPS

- Be on time for the interview; plan on arriving 15 minutes early.
- Know the interviewer's name and ask for them by name when you arrive for the interview.
- Do not wear slippers (Don't ask, just don't do it).
- Bring at least two copies of your resume and any attachments (Training certificates).
- Pen and paper, take notes.
- Bring three personal references, with full names, phone, and emails.
- If they asked for any other documents, bring those too.
- Follow-up the interview with a 'thank you' email or note.

What do you look for in a supervisor?

Look for someone who is willing to tell you their "why" of becoming a therapist. Why do they supervise? What clients do they enjoy working with? I like working with supervisors who are open, human and willing to push me out of my comfort zone, but also will be behind me. I would ask them "How closely will I be working with you? How many supervision hours will I be getting? What is your theoretical construct?" You do not have to have a supervisor with the same orientation as you. In fact, in my office, I learn from others especially when we do not share the same background. It is nice to have a supervisor who is familiar with your orientation and can work with you and "stretch" you some. I have had many supervisors in my career, and I have learned a great deal from each and every one. I have heard stories about bad supervisors, don't think you have to put up with bad supervision or personal abuse. You are an intern or associate, not an indentured servant. So, here is my personal "advisee's rights" list:

- To be treated with kindness and respect.
- Meetings to occur as scheduled and start on time.
- Receives support in your learning.
- A supervisor who offers guidance in a constructive manner.
- Develop a sense of humor. We all do tough stuff; a little laughter is healthy.
- Is interested in what you and other staff are doing.
- Has time for questions to be answered (within reason, don't be a pest).

You will be spending time with your supervisor for over a year, most likely. Make sure you have respect for them and that you feel respected in your position.

Check List of To Do Items

☐ *Write, write and write some more. Find your voice, also thing about repurposing content from school.*

☐ *Read books on marketing and business or listen to books.*

☐ *Listen to podcasts.*

☐ *Network everywhere, join professional associations and start making connections.*

☐ *Attend all free or low-cost training, keep a record.*

☐ *Take photos of everything, plants, landscapes, people (only by permission).*

☐ *Start defining who your ideal clients will be. Create your 10 Most Ask Questions F & Q (see page36).*

☐ *Keep family a number 1 priority.*

☐ *Look for an awesome internship.*

☐ *Interview your supervisor.*

☐ *Evaluate the counseling process.*

Helpful Resources for Your Practice That I have used

Anger Management:

- Counseling Recovery, http://www.counselingrecovery.com Michelle Pointon Farris, helps therapists work with angry clients. My clients have loved this program.

Blogging:
- Social Work Coach and Blogging Coach: http://socialworkcoaching.com/author/sharonm50/, Sharon Martin, LCSW

Coaches:

- PurpleCo. http://purpleco.com.au, Jo Muirhead

- The Counselor's Coach: https://www.thecounselorscoach.com, Mari A. Lee, LMFT, CSAT

- Zynnyme, https://www.zynnyme.com, Kelly Higdon, LMFT and Miranda Palmer, LMFT

Court:

- Therapist Court Prep: https://therapistcourtprep.com,If you need help with court or anything court related like subpoenas look up Nicol Stolar-Peterson, LCSW, BCD

Therapist Practice in a box

Grief Counseling Program:

- Your Path Through Grief, a compressive online support for those grieving. http://www.yourpaththroughgrief.com/, Jill Johnson-Young, LCSW

Paperwork Packets:

- QA Prep: https://www.qaprep.com, Maelisa Hall, Psy.D

- The Counselor's Coach: https://www.thecounselorscoach.com, Mari A. Lee, LMFT, CSAT

- Therapist Practice in a Box: https//www.therapistbox.com, Sherry Shockey-Pope

Private Practice Management Assistance:

- My Solution Services, Frances J. Harvey, C.P.C. and her team, can help you with a variety of services. From IT web design, answering phones, billing and practice management skills. http://www.mysolutionservices.com/

Videos:

- Fylmit. Com, https://www.fylmit.com/, Ernesto Segismundo, Jr.

I've Got Your Back......Really, I Do

I know this entire process of starting and staying in business is hard and sometimes the self-doubt overwhelms us. I know this because I have been in your shoes and I have been overwhelmed by my business, and there are at least a few times a year when I want to throw in the towel and call it quits. I don't call it quits, and I don't want you to either. That is why I have created the **_Implementation of The Box Program._** *www.therapistbox.com*

This program was designed to save you time and money by doing the things right the first time. This program will support and help you work through the hard "I want to quit times" that every business owner I know has been through.

I have designed this 12-week program that is just for you. It provides 6 weeks of direct information and a week in between to complete the homework and create that business of your dreams. This implementation package is broken down into (6) 90-minutes video calls where you and I really dive into your business. Each block is designed to build on the other and build your business fast. The detailed blocks consist of:

1. The mindset of creating a Business & The Nuts n' Bolts the Basics (Business assessment)

2. The Right Clients and where to Find them & Website Development

3. Website Development II & Marketing

4. Marketing II & Blog Development
5. Social Media & Videos
6. Fine Tuning Your Practice

For more information and to schedule your FREE consultation, please go to my website: therapistbox.com. and sign up. You will also find valuable information on that website as I am adding new things all the time.

I am looking forward to working with you on building your private practice of your dreams.

You Got This

Sherry

Let's Connect:

Social Media Links

Website: https://www.Therapistbox.com

Facebook: https://www.facebook.com/Slpope03/

LinkedIn: https://www.linkedin.com/in/sherry-shockey-pope-lmft-375b1225/

Instagram: https://www.instagram.com/sherry_shockey_pope_lmft/

Twitter: https://twitter.com/search?q=sherry+shockey-pope

References Cited

Ballard, C.G., O'Brien, J.T., Reichelt, K., Perry, E.K. (2002). Aromatherapy as a safe and effective treatment for the management of agitation in severe dementia: the results of a double-blind, placebo-controlled trial with Melissa. *Journal of Clinical Psychiatry, 63*, 553-8.

Bressi, C., Porcellana, M., Gambini, O., Madia, L., Muffatti, R., Peirones, Altamira, A. C. (2009). Burnout among psychiatrists in Milan: A multicenter survey. Psychiatric Services, 60(7), 985-988. Retrieved from http://neuro.psychiatryonline.org/data/Journals/PSS/3884/09ps985.pdf

Conrad P, Adams C. The effects of clinical aromatherapy for anxiety and depression in the high-risk postpartum woman - a pilot study. Complement Ther Clinical Practice. 2012 Aug;18(3):164-8. doi: 10.1016/j.ctcp.2012.05.002. Epub 2012 Jun 27.

Kasper S. An orally administered Lavandula oil preparation (Silexan) for anxiety disorder and related conditions: an evidence-based review. International J Psychiatry Clinical Practice. 2013 Nov 17 Supplemental 1:15-22. doi: 10.3109/13651501.2013.813555. Review. PMID:23808618

Lim, N., Kim, E. K., Kim, H., Yang, E., & Lee, S. M. (2010). Individual and work- 169 related factors influencing burnout of mental health professionals: A meta-analysis. Journal of

References Cited

Employment Counseling, 47(2), 86-96. doi:10.1002/j.2161-1920. 2010.tb00093.x

Millar, B & Moore, J. (2008). Successful topical treatment of hand warts in a pediatric patient with tea tree oil (Melaleuca alternifolia). *Complementary Therapies in Clinical Practice, 14*(4), 225- 27.

National Institute of Health: *Aromatherapy and Essential Oils (PDQ®)–Health Professional Version, April 21, 2016, Accessed 11/29/16* https://www.cancer.gov/about-cancer/treatment/cam/hp/aromatherapy-pdf.

Pew Research Center: Week of March 17- April 12, 2015.

The University of Minnesota, Center for Spiritual & Healing and Growth. Charlton Meadows (contributor Linda Halcon, Ph.D., MPH, RN) http://www.takingcharge.csh.umn.edu/explore-healing- practices/aromatherapy/how-do-essential-oils-work, July 16, 2016

U.S. Census Bureau Data, 2012.

Waldman, Larry, PH.D., *The Graduate Course You Never Had.* 2010 UCS Press Arizona

Walsh, Robert, MA, Dasenbrook, Norman, MS, *The Complete Guide to Private Practice for Licensed Mental Health Professionals*, 4th · edition, 1999.

Wax, Dustin, Lifehack, "How *to Be an Expert (and Find One if You're Not)"* accessed November 22, 2016, http://bit.ly/2gduomV.

Woelk, H & Schlafke, S. (2009). A multi-center, double-blind, randomized study of the Lavender oil preparation Silexan in comparison to Lorazepam for generalized anxiety disorder. *Phytomedicine, 17,* 94-99.

Therapist Practice in a Box
CEU Follow-up Test

Complete the following questions and forward the document to Sherry@therapistbox.com and then a 6-hour certificate will be emailed back to you.

1. Having the right mindset about building a private practice is important because?
   A. The world needs your services.
   B. Business skills can be learned
   C. Fear is just an emotion and will go away
   D. All of the above
   E. None of the above

2. Traits that all clinicians need to become a successful practice owner?
   A. Resiliency
   B. Focus
   C. Tenacity
   D. A vision
   E. Patience
   F. All of the above

3. Creating a Private Practice requires?
   A. A business license
   B. A lot of money
   C. Time
   D. A and C
   E. A vacation

221

4. A sole proprietor is?
    A. A business structure that has one person in the business
    B. Difficult to set up
    C. Costs a lot of money
    D. Not worth the time
    E. Not a real business

5. A fictitious name is?
    A. A funny way to spell your business
    B. Not needed for therapy businesses
    C. Tells customers who you are
    D. An assumed name, a trade name or DBA (Doing Business As)
    E. A good book

6. Having a website is not necessary because?
    A. Clients don't look on the internet
    B. Not worth the money
    C. Wait, a website is an absolute necessity
    D. It's hard to build
    E. Learning how to do it takes too much time
    F. None of the above

CEU follow-up test

7. Therapists should develop a niche market because?
   A. It cost less to market
   B. It makes marketing easier
   C. Clients want specialists and are willing to pay more for them
   D. Helps prevent therapist burnout
   E. All of the above ⟵

8. A business plan is not necessary because?
   A. A business plan is only used for a bank loan
   B. Therapist like to wing it
   C. Is silly and a waste of time
   D. Whoa, it's always needed as it is a written vision for where you want the business to go in the next couple of years; even a simple one would help with planning ⟵
   E. Is only for therapists that want to make $100,000 or more

9. When you consider finding a location for your business it's important to consider?
   A. The location of the office (neighborhood)
   B. The cost
   C. How you can maximize the space
   D. Sharing space with a trusted colleague
   E. All of the above ⟵

Therapist practice in a box

10. Branding your company is important because?
    A. It identifies your company to clients
    B. Only includes the use of stationary
    C. Don't worry about it you're a small company
    D. Includes a logo, colors, stationary, the vibe and the look and feel of a company.
    E. Is not important

11. Taking the number of sessions all client attends therapy and dividing it by the number of clients will give you?
    A. A headache
    B. The average of the cost to run your practice
    C. The average number of sessions your clients stay with you
    D. The average you should charge a client
    E. The value of each client

12. Once you have the average number of session a client is in therapy, you can determine
    A. How much to charge
    B. The client's lifetime value
    C. How many clients you need to have a full caseload
    D. A number to help determine your income projections, ROI, if your marketing efforts are worth it
    E. None of the above

CEU follow-up test

13. A profit margin is?
    - (A) A number that will tell you if you are making money (profit) or losing money (loss)
    - B. A number that will tell you to sell items
    - C. The number of gross profit
    - D. Is better left up to the CPA
    - E. Just another number

14. All therapists should have malpractice insurance if?
    - A. Therapists that take client insurance
    - B. Therapists that are self-insured or have their spouse's insurance
    - C. Therapist that have slip and fall insurance
    - (D) That assess, see or treat any clients in a therapeutic manner
    - E. None of the above

15. An NPI is
    - A. A number required by law
    - B. A number needed to file taxes
    - (C) A National Provider Number that is part of the HIPAA law
    - D. A useful number that you must purchase
    - E. All of the above

16. A good place to market includes:
    - A. Friends and family
    - B. Networking events
    - C. Social Media
    - D. Doctors and dentists
    - E. Anywhere your ideal client is
    - (F) All of the above

Therapist practice in a box

OPTIONAL:

17. What I found most helpful in this book was?

You sharing your experience

several options for same services

references & links

18. What I found least helpful?

not having sample forms

19. Name, License and email address (**Required for certificate**)

KATHLEEN E. MILLER, LCAC
LICENSE # 87001570A (Indiana)
Kathymiller951@yahoo.com

82655506R00134

Made in the USA
Lexington, KY
04 March 2018